Wolves of Russia

Part One:

Changing Landscapes

"For our freedom and yours."

(Dyslexia-friendly edition)

Published by Crossbridge Books
Worcester
www.crossbridgeeducational.com

© Crossbridge Books 2024

All rights reserved. No part of this publication
may be reproduced, stored in a retrieval system,
or transmitted in any form or by any means –
electronic, mechanical, photocopying, recording.
or otherwise – without prior permission of the
Copyright owner.

ISBN 978 1 913946 23 4

British Library Cataloguing in Publication Data
A catalogue record for this book is available from the
British Library

Wolves of Russia

Part One:

Changing Landscapes

(Dyslexia-friendly edition)

R M Mace

'The wolf also shall dwell with the lamb,
The leopard shall lie down with the young goat,
The calf and the young lion and the fatling together,
And a little child shall lead them.
The cow and bear shall graze,
Their young ones shall lie down together,
And the lion shall eat straw like the ox.'

Isaiah 11:6-9

CONTENTS: Page:

Foreword v

Prologue to Part One vi

Part 1 – Changing Landscapes

Chapter 1 – The calm before the storm (Summer 1914) 2

Chapter 2 – In the service of the Tsar (1914) 13

Chapter 3 – The Tsar takes command (1915) 24

Chapter 4 – Close encounters (1916) 35

Chapter 5 – Revolution and escape (1917) 48

Chapter 6 – Return to Kiev (1917) 65

Chapter 7 – The Polish Army (1918) 80

Chapter 8 – In the service of the Marshal (1919) 95

Chapter 9 – Return to Rovno (1920) 111

Author's note on Part One and copy of transcripts 117

Biographies of notable people 123

Additional Historical Sources 125

FOREWORD:

This book is based on the memoirs of a very dear friend of the family who gave his name as: Vincent Viktor Rudolf. Viktor's father died when he was just sixteen, so the early part of this story, though based on his recollections and true accounts, has been reconstructed using historical archives to fill in the 'missing gaps'.

Viktor gave his family name as Rewicz (or Rawicz), as this is the name that he says the family used after the Revolution. Although this can be a family name, there are several noble families of differing names, who have the right to bear this coat of arms. The Rawicz coat of arms is one of the oldest in Poland. According to legend, King Canute of England left his crown and property to his son, but his goods and chattels (the moveable property) to his daughter. His son, the prince, ordered that a black bear, belonging to his father, be placed in the princess' chamber, hoping to inherit the whole estate. The princess tamed the bear and rode out of her bedchamber on its back. The story goes that she later married a Duke of Lorraine taking her inheritance with her. She gave her descendants a coat of arms with a girl riding a bear depicted on it. The coat of arms was called Rawicz. It symbolises the ability to overcome difficulties with honour; to change confusion into victory.

Viktor circa 1939

PROLOGUE TO PART ONE

I, Viktor, can still hear the chilling howl of those wolves today, all these years later; piercing, yet strangely muffled by the deep Siberian snow. At the age of ninety-eight, my hearing is not so good, and my forever-beautiful wife must often repeat herself. But some sounds stay with you, just as clear and soul-wrenching as the first time you hear them. My grandma called me 'Rudi' which in Polish means 'famous wolf'.

To really understand my story, you need to know my father's story too. He wasn't the sort of man to dwell on the past, and he didn't waste the precious time that he had at home with his family talking about a world that had changed forever. Over the years, growing up and picking up bits and pieces from aunts, uncles, and grandparents, I pieced together some of his life from before my sister and I were born. If he had sat down one day and told me his story, it might have gone something like this.

Viktor 2019

*Dedicated to the dear memory of my mother,
Eileen Margaret Anne Mohr (1931-2022)*

*"Believe in God and He will be in your heart".
(Viktor November 2022)*

PART ONE

CHANGING LANDSCAPES

(1914-1923)

My father's story.
If he had written it down, it might have gone something like this...

Rawicz coat of arms

CHAPTER 1

THE CALM BEFORE THE STORM (SUMMER 1914)

Father's old horse-drawn carriage trundled around the courtyard in front of the turquoise blue and cream Mariyins'kyi Palace, surrounded by forest, high on a plateau overlooking the city of Kiev. Here in the palace, the Governor, Nikolai Sukovkin, was having a small social gathering. As we approached the palace, circuiting the formal gardens laid out at the front, and continuing to the steps outside the entrance, I could see several motor cars that were already parked near the entrance, and, not for the first time, I wished that father would find that he could afford to buy one. The family of one of my friends, a fellow student at university in St Petersburg, owned a Latvian-made Russo-Balt automobile and had shown it off just before we went down for the summer break. But father was old school and preferred real 'horsepower'. He still proudly kept the coat of arms emblazoned on the carriage door and Piotr, our coachman, who knew how to crack his whip, still wore the family livery when escorting the family to formal events.

I jumped down from the carriage and turned to hand my mother down just as an elegant Delaunay-Belleville swept into view, the roar of the engine unsettling the horses.

"I can't think why you like those machines Janusz," said mother with undisguised disgust, "they make such a dreadful noise; even the snort of a bull seems more musical to me." We were not acquainted with the occupant and continued up the stone steps into the Mariyins'kyi Palace without introductions.

"I'm sure you would find the ride exhilarating and far more comfortable than an old carriage; it's just that the noise is unfamiliar. I don't think it's any louder than a team of horses pounding the road," I commented as we handed hats and coats to the waiting footmen. As their only son, it always fell to me to accompany my mother at these functions whilst father did the rounds, greeting the various local dignitaries, civil and military, that had gathered.

The July evening was sultry and despite the quantity of large windows that lit the room on three levels high up into the lavishly painted vaulted ceiling, none of them would be opened and the air was stuffy. There seemed to be an uneasy atmosphere in the room, something not quite tangible. As Mother glanced around, deciding to whom she would like me to take her, I found myself staring abstractedly at the highly polished marble floor with its intricate geometric patterns reflecting the many electric lights that had been installed.

The Governor of Kiev, Nikolai Sukovkin, and the former Governor, Count Pavel Nikolayevich Ignatiev, were standing with a small group of men in one of the balconied and curtained alcoves near the top of one of the curving stairways that led up to the gallery. The conversation was apparently lively and intense and there were one or two raised voices, unusual for a merely social evening. Political intrigue and the restlessness of the working people seemed to have become the staple diet of every topic for debate in the last few months especially amongst the better educated classes. Like my father, I did not trust politicians or economists and did my best to avoid such discussions.

My thoughts turned to the last few weeks that I had spent taking leisurely boat trips on the Dnieper River with friends, and escorting pretty girls to the parks and merry-go-rounds, parties in the Merchant's Garden, evenings at the theatre, even squeezing in a trip to the old caves at the Pecherskaya Monastery to admire the most recent gifts from the Imperial Family. It had been amusing, but the social life of Kiev did not interest me. Now I was looking forward to heading back to St Petersburg to continue my Architectural study at the Institute of Civil Engineers and wondered briefly if we would be studying designs for marble floors like the one at which I was gazing.

"There, take me to see Princess Natalia Nikolayevna Meshcherkaya, Jan, she is waiting to speak to me. She looks quite agitated," hissed my mother in a rather loud attempt at a whisper. The Princess, the wife of the former Governor, was standing amongst a small group of animated ladies at the foot of the other curved stairway, where palms, plants, and a profusion of flowers had been tastefully arranged. I prepared myself for the inevitable boredom of listening to society gossip, probably about whether the Grand Duchess Olga Nikolaievna would be marrying into the Romanian royal family.

"Try not to look bored Janusz," admonished Mother as we strolled towards the group that did admittedly seem unusually excited.

"Countess, have you heard the news from Petersburg?" asked Natalia Nikolayevna breathlessly and continued without waiting for a reply, "There has been an attack on the 'starets' Rasputin, and we have heard that his life is in danger. He had gone to Siberia a fortnight ago, and on his arrival at his own village, he was attacked and stabbed by a young woman!"

"The wound might be fatal," interjected Anna Ilyinichna Korsakova, a young lady distantly related to one of Kiev's former Governors, in a voice that held a distinct hint of hope. There were many who secretly hoped that Russia would at last be delivered from the baneful influence of the self-styled peasant priest, but they dare not reveal their feelings openly, although it was well known what Maria Feodorovna, the Dowager Empress, felt about the influence of that man over her son the Tsar and her daughter-in-law the Tsarina. I left Mother with her friends and wandered off in search of more entertaining conversation.

Amongst the guests I spotted the full and ruddy face of the Chief of Staff Alexander Sergeyevich Lukomsky and his wife Sophia Mikhailovna in conversation with Nikolai Nikolaevich Dukhonim, the commander of the Forty Second Infantry Division in Kiev. He was a fascinating man who always had romantic stories to tell of his time operating as a secret agent in Austria. The ends of his moustache were twirled up into ringlets and he wore a small goatee under his lower lip and pince-nez perched on his nose. His voice was thin but melodious, but perhaps more fascinating to a young man was his wife, Natalia Vladimirovna. She was stately and beautiful, with a glowing blush, and dark, thick, curly hair.

Father escorted Mother into supper, and I found myself next to a lively young lady who was happy to talk banalities all through the meal and I was happy to let her, thus allowing myself to let my own thoughts drift away without the effort of having to reply. After supper I joined some other young men for cards and successfully managed to dodge the stronger liquor with which we were being generously regaled. Later, on our way back to the family estate, father, speaking in Polish, expressed his concern about the rumours that were circulating in Kiev and, according to one or two persons who had been present that evening, also at Moscow and possibly even at St Petersburg.

"People are saying that trouble is brewing with Austria and that is why the French President, M. Poincaré, is coming to St Petersburg to discuss the situation with the Tsar," said my father with a note of anxiety in his voice. "We can't expect that there will be no consequences to the assassination of the Archduke Franz Ferdinand in Sarajevo last month."

"As if there isn't enough trouble here in Kiev," put in Mother, adding, "the papers say there have been numerous strikes since January, and I know there has been some unrest in our mills, even though your father thinks he has hidden it from me." The rest of the journey home was thankfully taken up by more domestic issues, on which subjects I was at that time blissfully uninvolved, such as the prospective purchase of a new steam engine to power the grain mill. I was able to spend the journey gazing appreciatively out of the carriage window at the familiar landscape.

The area immediately around our house was very attractive, with ponds and meadows stretching across on the lower ground, while beyond, the fields were enveloped by wooded hills. I loved to wander alone in the beautiful old pine forests and surround myself with the wildness of nature. There were often wolves in the area at that time, worrying and sometimes savaging the sheep and cattle; I had joined in with a hunt when I had been home in the Spring. Beaters had been drafted in from the village and spread out in the forest, moving forward, and making a din with wooden rattles. Once, as a boy, during the school holidays, when I was alone in the forest, I heard something rustling and turned around to see who was there. Just beyond a fir tree I could see an enormous he-wolf. Thankfully I had remembered to take my whistle, as instructed by my father to always carry if alone in the forest and blew it as hard as I could. I was only a few steps from the wolf and dared not move, but at the sound of the whistle, the wolf turned and slowly loped away, disappearing into the trees, as I ran the few miles home as fast as my legs would carry me. As the carriage pulled up and the steps were let down by Piotr, I was jolted back to the present.

The next day, Father and I rode out to one of the lakes on the estate. We kept a small boat moored to an old wooden pier and we rowed out a good way to see if we could catch some fish. I remember how peaceful and quiet it was. The air hardly moved and there were no ripples on the surface of the water. We caught a few small trophies for our efforts. I had always preferred fishing to hunting although of course I was an excellent shot, but fishing was so much quieter and more relaxing. I remember father dozed off briefly, his head dropping suddenly onto his chin, waking him up. He looked up into the sky, took a deep breath, and spoke what later seemed prophetic words.

"The calm before the storm Janusz. We had better be getting back or I shall be in trouble with your mother for keeping you to myself." He wasn't a man to question, and I took the oars in hand, rowing with long deep strokes while he watched appreciatively. We ambled slowly back taking the forest path through tall straight oaks and grassy glades and skirting the farmland nearer home. As we approached, we passed a group of about twenty or so peasant women who had been haying on the estate and had come for some refreshment. They stood back to let us pass. With their plain headscarves, long skirts of heavy home-spun cloth and aprons looking somehow like uniforms, and holding their long hay forks in front, they put me in mind of soldiers on parade.

Having taken the horses to their stabling we went into the house - referred to as a palace by the local people but more of a rambling manor with a few turrets added for good measure - to change our soiled clothes, both silently absorbed by our own thoughts. We were met by Father's man Sowiński who informed us that Mother could be found in the 'blue supper room' as she liked to call it. This loyal old man with his leathery skin and bushy eyebrows had been with the family since he himself had been a boy; he was part of the furniture. I had always liked him and had often turned to him for help when I had got into a scrape as a boy. I caught the twinkle in his eye and smiled back at him. It's curious how events that seem ordinary and trivial at the time can become so vivid in memory when they precede significant events.

I went to my room and changed into formal evening wear and joined my parents shortly after. Having married young, Mother was only in her thirties and still very beautiful. She wore a sapphire blue gown with lashings of old lace, a string of sapphires at her throat, and sapphires in her rings, thus perfectly coordinated with the furnishings in her favourite room. Father was tall, slim, and gracious in his bearing but self-assured and still surprisingly strong. He entered the room with his customary stride, giving Mother an old-fashioned kiss on the hand and presenting his cheek for her to kiss that always made her giggle.

There were no guests that evening, so our meal was simple; it wasn't long before the servants had removed the covers and left us in peace. Mother played the piano, a beautiful ebony Art Nouveau Diederichs upright made by Russians in St Petersburg, while Father perused a journal. Mother had begun playing a lively mazurka and then suddenly stopped as if she had recalled something important.

"Come, get your violin out, play with me Jan, you can't have forgotten." After a brief search I found my violin case, tightened the bow, rubbed it gently with the rosin, and tuned up. At this point Father put the journal down to listen, sitting back and closing his eyes.

"Your father always gets melancholy when we play together Jan, I miss this most when you are away," said Mother wistfully. We played a few waltzes together and finished with a mournful nocturne – Chopin of course. I remember in later years being glad that I had stayed with them that evening. As she played the final melancholy chord Mother stood up and said,

"It must be time for the tea tray." Social visits were often made at nine o'clock in the evening, so the tea tray was always made ready for any unexpected guests. It was duly brought in, the enormous elaborately decorated tea urn, the samovar, carried separately by one of the stronger servants. Glasses of tea, in their silver stands with elegant handles, were dispensed, Father taking his usual spoonful of jam stirred in; I prefer a lump of sugar. Mother nibbled on a dainty cake while father searched through a plate of bonbons. That comfortable picture is still perfectly clear in my mind to this day.

The next day, we heard that Austria had presented an ultimatum to Serbia. The language in the press was extremely angry and over the next few days the tone became increasingly violent. The press accused Austria of wanting to annihilate Serbia which Russia of course could not allow – the national honour was at stake. The next we heard was that Austria had ordered general mobilisation and had begun the bombardment of Belgrade. We found out later that marshal law had been declared in Kiev and the Ukrainian paper, the Rada, had been closed. The next news arrived too soon to fully comprehend the events that were happening in Europe.

I had planned out a route of about five miles, to include the old orchard with its mulberry trees, to give myself a decent hike through the forest. Taking my loaded revolver in case of any unfriendly encounters, I had set off at a brisk pace looking forward to the exercise. I had not gone more than two hundred yards before I heard someone calling. Sowiński was waving his arms and beckoning me back to the house. I hurried back fearful that something might have happened to Mother or Father and found them in Father's study. Father was pacing backwards and forwards muttering under his breath, something about the dammed Prussians.

"Germany has declared war on Russia, Janusz," Mother whispered, "We are at war."

I can't remember now exactly when it arrived, but I vividly remember the sinking feeling in the pit of my stomach as I read the order for me immediately to go to St Petersburg where I would be a member of the Imperial Reserve Bodyguard, the Cossack Regiment of the Konvoy, whose sole purpose was to protect the Imperial family. As the son of a nobleman, it was my duty to undertake either military or civil service. Many years ago, Peter the Great had decreed that noble families had to send their sons into service or forfeit their land and property to the crown. My father had no choice but to send me into service. Before the war this could be as a civilian — as an architect, graduating with rank eleven, the equivalent of a staff captain of cavalry. But with the outbreak of war, the Tsar naturally sent his most experienced men to the front and needed educated well-born men for his bodyguard. I had been summoned to a specially selected elite Cossack unit, originally created in the early nineteenth century, to guard the Tsar.

The next day I left home for the capital.

CHAPTER 2

IN THE SERVICE OF THE TSAR (1914)

The fiery red Cossack coat hung heavily about my legs. The shashka, the ceremonial sabre, plus the silver ornamented qama dagger at my waist felt irksome. Along with hundreds of other officers, I was standing in the Nicholas Hall, the ballroom of the Winter Palace, in St Petersburg. I glanced up at the enormous chandeliers, wondering momentarily how safe the fixtures were to carry what must have been an incredible weight. Gradually, I became aware of a rising tide of noise from the crowd of thousands that had gathered in the square outside. Catching me off guard, Nikolai Sergeyevich, one of my fellow officers, thumped me on the shoulder, speaking with barely contained excitement and using my Russian name.

"Hey! Ivan Ivanovich, what are you dreaming of? Is it your sweetheart in a ballgown? Do you hear that noise outside? The people are cheering."

The Emperor, Empress, and the royal family had arrived at St Petersburg by sea and walked across the Palace Square through the waving crowds. They then processed into the Winter Palace, slowly making their way through the throng of officers that swarmed up the stairs and in all the great halls. There was a hush in the Hall as we waited for the arrival of the Tsar. Somewhere in the distance we could hear the tremulous voice of a priest as he sang the service of Moleban - a prayer of intercession for the people and the Tsar of Holy Russia - in the small church along the corridor. Reverently, we removed our hats and hung our heads in prayer. As a Polish Roman Catholic, I was content to share in the prayers of the people.

When the short service was over, their Majesties and the Royal family entered the Nicholas Hall with calm, gracious smiles. There was an expectant silence as we waited to hear The Emperor speak. Outside, the crowd was temporarily subdued. the Tsar's declaration of war manifesto was read by a member of the Imperial Suite, and then the Tsar spoke directly to us in an unrehearsed speech. At first his voice seemed to shake from nervousness, but as he continued, he became more confident, and I sensed the mounting inspiration in the crowd. He finished with rousing words:

"We will not end this war until every last enemy is driven out of the Russian land."

There was a deafening roar as we all cheered and waved our hats, completely caught up in the moment. Ignoring the usual court etiquette, the Emperor and Empress walked through the crowded hall, the royal family and the rest of their entourage following in their wake. As they passed through, soldiers fought to kiss their hands. I had seen the Tsar many times before, but in this melee, surrounded by both battle-hardened soldiers and raw recruits, he appeared the epitome of gentleness, a quiet but confident little man. He was, in fact, roughly the same height as me and I was generally considered to be on the small side for a Cossack.

The procession carried on through the pressing mass of bodies and reached the Malachite Hall with its stunning green columns. I happened to glance across at our commanding officer General Count Alexander Grabbe, who was beginning to look a little agitated. Of course, the Tsar was discreetly surrounded by secret police, but as His Majesty's Own Cossack Escort, our presence should be clearly visible. I grabbed Nikolai Sergeyevich by the arm and pointed towards the balcony, in which direction the Tsar and royal family appeared to be headed. I shouted in his ear,

"Nikolai Sergeyevich, do you want promotion?"

"Who doesn't? What do you have in mind?" he shouted back. In reply I pointed to Count Grabbe and then in the direction of the balcony. He nodded in acknowledgement and together we pushed our way closer, dragging a few fellow officers with us to create a protective wall of Cossacks behind the royal family as they emerged onto the balcony.

It was an unforgettable scene. As the Tsar appeared, the entire sea of people in the Palace Square, as one body, got down on their knees in front of him. The thousands of flags that had been waving were lowered and then they began to sing the national anthem 'God save the Tsar'. It began like a slow chant, a prayer, the sound rising and falling like the swell of the ocean, and despite my Polish heritage, I was moved to tears by the strength of emotion.

After the ceremony, as members of His Majesty's Own Cossacks, we escorted the imperial family back to their residence. The Tsar preferred to live at Alexander Palace, built by Catherine the Great, about twenty kilometres from the city of St Petersburg, in Tsarskoe Selo - the Tsar's village. Our convoy swept through the village, skirting the lakes, parks, canals, and flower gardens, and halted at the entrance to the wing of the palace where the family had their private rooms, before returning to the barracks. The barracks where we were quartered were not far from the Alexander Palace within the boundaries of Tsarskoe Selo.

As we approached the long line of the building with its square turrets at regular intervals stretching into the distance, I wondered, as I had often done before, why the sky always seemed so blue up here on the tideless north coast. The August evening sun was low in the sky casting long shadows. The flat green meadows stretched into the horizon following the line of the low grey building; the trees were all still in leaf. War had been proclaimed but the sun still shone, the grass still grew, the birds still sang, and the sky was still blue.

A few days later, I was sleeping in my bunk, in the deep slumber that goes with a clear conscience and no responsibilities. I was rudely awakened by Nikolai Sergeyevich, tossing his boot at me.

"Our illustrious Commander-in-Chief, Nicholas Nicolaievitch, has brought their Majesties their first trophy – a machine gun captured from the Germans in East Prussia," he said as if he had been speaking about someone coming back with a purchase from the market. This was the first skirmish about which we had news and I wondered how many Russian - or Polish - lives this 'trophy' had cost.

Not long after this, we were on board the Imperial train bound for Moscow, where the Tsar, according to tradition, would ask God's blessing on himself and the people.

"Do you know Moscow well? Do you think we'll get time off to find a decent kabak to get drunk in?" asked Nikolai Sergeyevich, drowsy from the tiresome journey. I told him that I had been a few times but doubted that we would get any leave. I spoke my thoughts aloud.

"It seems strange to be having all these parades, all this pomp and ceremony, when we are already at war."

"It's for the morale of the troops and the populace, Ivan Ivanovich, to make people willing to lay down their lives for the Little Father and Holy Russia," came the sleepy response as he shut his eyes and promptly dozed off, his long limbs draped carelessly over the seat. I found myself liking this tall young Cossack who was used to a more rural way of life than ours. I tried to imagine him being introduced to my parents. My father would probably try to challenge his knowledge of the world but then accept him at face value. My mother would probably think him too unrefined and behave towards him with the impeccable politeness she always showed to those whom she really did not care for.

The train began to slow as the outlying villages north of Moscow came into view. We rumbled across bridges, over rivers, skirting lakes and slowing down as we reached the suburbs. The juddering of brakes saved me the job of waking Nikolai who got leisurely to his feet and peered out of the window.

"It looks much like any other city to me – maybe a few more churches than I have seen before," he complained.

"I think you'll be impressed by the Kremlin Nikolai Sergeyevich," I offered, adding with a wry smile, "there are even more churches and cathedrals in there; they say there are forty times forty churches in Moscow, all with bells."

"Then, Ivan Ivanovich, we shall have to be on the lookout for devout young Muscovite girls!" he laughed back.

Having carried out our duty during the reception at the station, we followed the long file of carriages towards the Kremlin. An enormous crowd had gathered in the squares and streets. People had even climbed on the rooftops and up into the trees. They hung out of windows, filled the balconies, and seemed to swarm out of every orifice. The church bells were ringing as if they would never stop. Nikolai gave me a sideways glance, rolling his eyes. I admit my lip twitched but I managed to keep a straight face.

In a rerun of the St Petersburg event, thousands of people spontaneously opened their mouths and out poured the national anthem, overwhelming in its religious grandeur and emotion. The procession was led by priests in gold vestments holding great crucifixes in both hands. The cavalcade arrived at the Iberian Gate where their Majesties got out and went into the chapel. The Grand Duchesses as usual were all dressed in identical, but simple, outfits. The poorly Tsarevitch, suffering and unable to walk that day from his haemophilia, was carried by a huge Cossack who lifted him high so that he could be seen by the cheering crowds.

Behind his sleepy look and droopy eyelids, Nikolai was looking intently around with the wariness of a hunted animal. For decades the royal family had been subjected to assassinations and attempted assassinations – the terror threat was real and at these occasions at their most likely – and we were tasked with their protection. They re-emerged and walked slowly back to their carriage and the procession resumed, under the old gate and into the Kremlin. Over the next few days there were more of these ceremonial processions to cathedrals for mass, to monasteries for prayers, and the population swarmed in support of The Emperor wherever he went.

A week later we were back at the Tsarskoe Selo barracks near the capital, that had now been renamed Petrograd in an anti-German gesture. From then on, life seemed to consist of travel – seemingly endless train journeys. As the Tsar's personal escort, his bodyguard, we had to follow him around as he travelled the country, to General Headquarters at Mogilev, visiting the troops, visits to the front, to clearing stations, military hospitals, and factories, and back to barracks. Sometimes we were escorting just the Tsar and sometimes it included other members of the royal family. We were part of a handful of Cossacks brought in to serve the Imperial family, and at official, or ceremonial, occasions the Tsar wore our Kuban Cossack uniform. As the winter months drew on, not only the landscape changed, with the sepia effect of forests, with tall straight silver birch trees, against miles of level snow, but the colour seemed to seep out of clothing as all the men donned their military uniforms and the ladies transformed themselves into nurses. Nikolai's sense of humour kept some zest in the dull routine of our life.

"A rabbit was running like crazy through the forest and met a wolf," began Nikolai, launching into one of his many jokes and using different voices for those speaking, a gruff voice for the wolf and a peculiar falsetto for the rabbit. "The wolf asked the rabbit, 'What's the matter? Why the haste?' The rabbit stopped to answer, saying, 'The camels in the forest are being caught and shod.' 'But you're not a camel,' said the wolf. 'After you're caught and shod, just you try proving that you are not a camel,' replied the rabbit." Nikolai chuckled at his own joke. I laughed with him and then, imitating Nikolai's gruff voice, added,

"Would you like me to help you prove that you're not a camel?' asked the wolf and then kindly ate the rabbit." Nikolai enjoyed my addition, thumped me in the chest in congratulation, and gave a crack of laughter.

It was one of Nikolai's endearing characteristics, that he could remember an old joke at just the right moment. He had explained soon after we met that in his large family, there was an unspoken, ongoing competition to be the one who could tell the most jokes. This large family, as far as I could make out, consisted of two older siblings, one a brother in the Horse Guards, the other a sister already married, and three younger siblings, as well as numerous cousins, aunts, and uncles. His experience of talking with younger children and young ladies, made him a favourite with the Grand Duchesses, especially Grand Duchess Maria Nikolaievna who even knew his name.

When the wounded from the front began to arrive at Tsarskoe Selo, we often saw the Tsarina and the two oldest Grand Duchesses, dressed in their 'Sisters of Mercy' uniforms. They had all trained and qualified as surgical nurses at the outbreak of war and even helped with the most traumatic of operations. The Grand Duchesses always had a shy smile for their officers.

Once, in the barracks, Nikolai swung his heavy long black cloak across his shoulders in a swirling motion just as I bent to collect mine that had been draped across the back of a chair. The corner of the cloak caught me full in the face and dragged into my eye. I yelped from the shock, and partly because I was bent over, the sound came out rather like a squeal.

"Little pig!" shouted Nikolai, "Ivan Ivanovich, you squealed like a pig!"

"You idiot, you could have taken out my eye," I replied crossly, but Nikolai had begun laughing and his laugh was always infectious, and I found myself joining in.

"Do you know that we call my youngest brother Little Pig?" he said catching his breath between guffaws.

"Enlighten me, I'm sure this will be a good story, true or not," I replied affably. He stroked his chin as he always did when about to tell a story and I could never really tell whether he was genuinely trying to recall an event or hurriedly making it up. But it was invariably entertaining, so worth the wait.

"A few years ago," he began, "around about harvest, all of us children were out playing in one of the apple orchards. We decided to help the peasants who were collecting apples. The girls borrowed some of those long billowy aprons that the ladies wear so that they could catch the apples that we threw down. Of course, we boys climbed up into the tree to shake the apples loose. The apples came down in a great shower and the girls, instead of catching the apples, ran away from the bombardment. One of the old ladies scolded us for bruising and wasting apples, telling us boys to get down and help collect the ones that had fallen. Being tall, I dropped quite easily back to the ground as did my older brother, but the youngest, as he lowered himself down caught his breeches on a gnarled stump on an old branch. When he let go of the branch he had been holding on to, he found himself suspended in mid-air by his breaches. Well, he squealed just like a little pig. Eventually his breeches tore, and he fell into the grass, and we have all called him Little Pig ever since." I wondered what it would be like to have brothers and even sisters – girls were still a great mystery to me at that time.

The steady stream of wounded continued. We heard that in East Prussia we had been defeated at Tannenberg and at the Masurian Lakes. In Galicia, we had captured Lemburg and were making advances, and we had resisted the Germans at Warsaw. When the Tsar went to General Headquarters at Mogilev, we went too, lodged in the local courthouse. The Tsarevich often accompanied him and slept on a camp bed in the Tsar's room. The Tsar's accommodation at Mogilev, the residence of the Governor situated on the summit of the steep left bank of the Dnieper River, was too small to accommodate the rest of the Imperial family. When the Tsarina and the Grand Duchesses came to visit, they lived in the Imperial train.

As we travelled along the front, we encountered increasing numbers of refugee families fleeing the German advance and heading for the safety of Moscow. We had heard about the tragedy of the town of Kalisz that had been completely destroyed by the Prussian army in the early stages of the conflict. This had caused great panic and fear, especially amongst the Polish and Lithuanian populations. We saw groups of people with scared faces and eyes full of tears; mothers shepherding their children to safety as best they could, hoping to find food and medicines to buy for their journey. Moscow, we were able to reassure them, had no shortages, and apart from the constant stream of wounded, no other signs of the war.

Special training was provided for non-commissioned officers who had an acknowledged right to this by education or birth. As a result, many officers who were sent to the front to replace those lost only had a few months preparation — Nikolai Sergeyevich and I fell into this category. For us it seemed that we were watching and waiting, waiting for some change, for some great upheaval.

CHAPTER 3

THE TSAR TAKES COMMAND (1915)

The early September climate at Mogilev, northwest of Kiev, was still very mild, it would be another month before the temperature would tumble and snow would begin to fall. Taking a short off-duty leave, Nikolai Sergeyevich and I were enjoying a hike through the nearby pine forest. There was no wind, and the air was still. The moisture from a drizzling mist collected into drops on bare twigs and dropped onto the freshly fallen leaves. It seemed strange to me to think that here everything was so still and peaceful while not too far away men were being subjected to the horrors of war. We were both busy with our own thoughts, hearing only the sound of our boots crunching on the fallen pinecones.

We suddenly became aware that the ground beneath us was rumbling and that the cause of this disturbance was approaching rapidly. My first thought was that somehow the war had suddenly come unexpectedly upon us, and a wave of adrenaline washed over me before I recognised the familiar sound of stampeding horses.

Heading towards us, coming down the track at breakneck speed, were half a dozen bearded Cossacks, thundering over the level ground at a terrific pace. When they saw us, they began to whoop, as it seemed to me, with the sheer joy of what was evidently a race. They passed us at full gallop as we leapt out of their way. The race apparently over, they returned at a canter. One of the

Cossacks was riding standing on his saddle, waving a handkerchief, presumably the winner. Another was in the process of crawling under the belly of his horse as he rode by. The sturdy ponies were trained to perfection; they stopped dead at a word from the riders.

"You know they can do all of that at full gallop," said Nikolai admiringly, "and aim and shoot accurately while they're doing it, and I have heard that at a word the ponies will lie down for their riders to give them shelter while they fire over the saddles," he added.

Naturally, we admired these courageous men who seemed to have been born on horseback, but the world was changing and so were the methods of warfare. 'What can horses do against machine guns?' I wondered, not sharing my thoughts aloud. I had learned to ride at a very young age. Once Father had taught me the basics, it was mostly old Sowiński who rode out with me to learn the way of horses. It always felt to me that horse riding came naturally; horses never shied away from me and invariably seemed to trust me. As if reading my thoughts, Nikolai said mockingly,

"You have a good seat yourself for such a short Cossack."

We had ridden out together when we first arrived. The horses had stepped over the still muddy fields as if over deep-pile carpet, and we had splashed into puddles between the furrows. We had galloped out of the woods and seen a pack of young wolves, already bigger than dogs. We reined in to look and I noticed that Nikolai, despite his long limbs, sat confidently on his black mare, reining her in without effort with his long fingers and firm hand. I wondered then how Nikolai would face a real enemy.

The news from the front had been steadily worsening. The Tsar, when we saw him now, instead of the lithe athletic figure, with his boyish countenance and clear blue eyes, was drawn and pale, his hair becoming thin and grey. There had been a steady retreat in front of the Prussian army, and in August, Warsaw, in Russian Poland, had been abandoned, and our troops had withdrawn to the right bank of the Vistula. By the end of August, the whole government of Poland was in the hands of the Germans.

The Cossack riders were now out of sight and out of earshot; the stillness and the mist closed back in, the quiet seeming somehow more intense and my thoughts all the louder in my head.

"What do you think Nikolai Sergeyevich, will the loss of Warsaw be our Austerlitz or our Borodino?" I wondered aloud.

"What are you talking about?" Nikolai asked nonplussed.

"If it's Austerlitz, we may recover, if Borodino then the Germans will reach Moscow," I explained, "haven't you read Tolstoy?"

"Read! Are you joking? You must know that it's shameful for a Cossack to occupy themselves with learning, especially reading," laughed Nikolai. By this time, we had reached the edge of a field where brown strips of winter rye grew, alternating with reddish strips of buckwheat and the pale-yellow stubble left from the summer wheat. A large hare lolloped by, it's summer coat already beginning to change into its white winter mantle.

"What? No jokes about a hare?" I asked innocently. Nikolai paused and stroked his chin, humming tunelessly for half a minute, then smiled and said,

"Did you know this is the anniversary of the hare inventing winter camouflage? Not that anyone noticed!" It took a moment for me to digest, but if Nikolai expected a reaction, he was disappointed. I became distracted by the sight of another person. In the gully, that ran along the same edge of the field following the line of the trees, was a woman. She was wearing the headscarf and bold-printed skirts worn by the local villagers in Saltanovka. She was clearly hunting for something among the undergrowth. Her frantic, darting movements were suggestive of fear, and we instinctively looked around for signs of danger. We moved closer and realised that she was calling a name.

"Have you lost someone?" called Nikolai. "Can we help?"

"My child, my little child," wailed the distraught woman. "She has wandered off... I was cooking... I only took my eyes off her for a moment... oh my baby... the wolves... what about the wolves?" She was so distressed we could hardly understand her. Evidently her young child had wandered away, and she was terrified that wolves, or other wild beasts, had taken her little daughter. I told Nikolai to stay with the woman while I went for help to get up a search party and hurried back to our quarters.

"Be quick, Ivan Ivanovich; this woman is going out of her mind; I find her wailing more terrifying than a pack of wolves," Nikolai called after me.

About a dozen of us managed to work out a circular area of roughly five miles across where the toddler might have got to. A neighbour stayed with the poor child's terrified mother. We scoured the area for many hours on foot, looking into every possible hiding place or den. As the hours dragged on, the situation began to seem more hopeless. I remember thinking how ironic it was that so many military men were searching to rescue one small child while the war would be indiscriminately killing thousands of unknown children who were just as precious to their families. I wish I could say that I had found the child, but it was another soldier who saw a piece of clothing fluttering under a bush, and found the child curled up, soaked to the skin, and unconscious but breathing. She was restored to her grateful mother. We later learned that the little girl had made a full recovery and had no recollection of the incident.

Meanwhile, I had a very different encounter out there in the forest during the search for the missing child. I had walked along the edge of the wood in the direction of some old oaks that rose out of the damp gully, slipping on the wet moss, and trying to look about me at the same time as watching where I trod. As I searched amongst the dense undergrowth, I came across a barely discernible animal track and followed it through a patch of long grass to a hollow in the bank. Amongst the tree roots, a tunnel had been dug out and I found myself looking at an unattended litter of wolf cubs and froze.

A she-wolf, who thought her cubs in danger, would not hesitate to attack.

Slowly, I began to back away, gingerly lowering the rifle from my shoulder. Out of the corner of my eye, out in the field on my left side, I saw her, the mother wolf. I raised my rifle and took aim, hoping all the while that I wouldn't have to shoot. She stood still for a moment watching me, then began moving towards me in a wide arc with a soundless lope. I followed her movements, keeping her in my sights, all the while taking slow steps backwards and hoping there were no others coming up behind me. Suddenly, she sprang forward and jumped over the gully. As she did so, I could see her grey back and her big reddish underbelly. She landed and paused, turning her heavy head to look at me, staring straight into my eyes as if trying to read my intention. Then she crouched, gnashed her teeth, and bounded away from me, into the trees, almost skidding to a halt in front of the nest. Here she turned and faced me with bared teeth. I heeded her warning and continued backing away. I continued to check behind me all the way until I had caught up with the others again, even though I knew the she wolf would only have attacked me to protect her young.

As more bad news was received from the front it filled us with foreboding. Our reverses in Poland had assumed catastrophic proportions, and we wondered if the invading horde would repeat the devastation of the Russian army that had been achieved by the French under Napoleon in 1812, causing us to withdraw, and abandon Russian land to the enemy. We knew that farms were short of labour and horses since they had all been shipped to the western or southern fronts. The cost of living in the towns and cities was rising. The food shortages were beginning to affect the cities, especially the capital, Petrograd, and it was beginning to have an impact on morale. It was at this point that the Tsar, believing it to be his solemn duty as head of state to assume the full burden of responsibility for the war effort, dismissed the Grand Duke Nicholas and took over as Supreme Commander.

As His Majesty's Escort continued to travel with the Tsar on his trips to review the troops, visit hospitals, and meet with his generals, we became increasingly aware of the impact of the invading army. The German army proceeded in a compact wave, sweeping everything before it in its passage, causing the entire population in the area to flee. The result was a constant flow of refugees, the numbers increasing with each battle. We began to see carts loaded with household goods, children, and old people, with cattle strung on; an unbroken river of people moving from west to east and blocking the highways. Then in October, our army gained a victory over the Austrians and the retreat halted. There was something of a lull over the winter; the Tsar went back to Tsarskoe Selo, and I went home for a short visit to my parents. Kiev was a simple train journey from Mogilev.

Sitting in her blue supper room, Mother was engrossed in a book as I entered unannounced. She was wearing a pale straw-coloured silk gown buttoned up to the throat; the elbow-length sleeves had ruffles of foaming cream lace that fell to her hands; the colours perfectly contrasted with the cornflower blue of her surroundings. She looked up at the sound of my footfall. At the sight of me, she threw the book aside and flew out of the chair to embrace me.

"Janusz! My darling boy," she began before recollecting that I was now a grown man who might not appreciate such a display of emotion. "How splendid you look in your uniform. Have you come to stay for long? Tell me everything," she continued sitting on the large sofa and patting the seat next to her invitingly. There wasn't much that I could tell her and kept to small talk.

"My friend, Nikolai Sergeyevich, is a great joker. He is much taller than me and I think the ladies prefer their Cossacks tall," I said, hoping to keep our conversation light.

"He sounds delightful; I hope you will introduce him to us one day," said Mother and then a cloud seemed to pass across her face. "Your father has gone with dear old Sowiński to try to calm the workers in the grain mill. Oh Janusz, the people are beginning to say such things, about anyone who owns land or property, no matter how well they have looked after the people on their estates. There seem to be troublemakers stirring up mischief everywhere you go." As she spoke, I became fascinated by a lock of her luxuriant chestnut brown hair that had escaped the bondage of the thick plait that she wound around her head like a crown. As she moved her head, the end of the curl would brush the corner of her eye and she would repeatedly push it away, distractedly trying to tuck it back into place. I soaked up the peace of that beloved room. The low autumn sun streaming through the long window and a fat black fly coming to the end of its life in the window embrasure. I wished I could stay and capture that moment on canvas and hang it on the wall to revisit again and again.

When Father came back, he took me into his study and told me that the political climate had changed in Kiev.

"You should see what they are writing in the press, the complaints are no longer just directed at the government, but they are criticising the Tsar himself since he has taken over command," he told me.

"But that is only to be expected," I pointed out. "We have had success in Austria and halted the invasion, the people will change their tune and put the Tsar back on his pedestal just as easily," I continued.

"Perhaps, but we have heard that there are rumours in Petrograd and Moscow that the Tsarina herself is a German spy. And," he added as if providing proof that the Imperial Court was in disarray, "Maria Feodorovna, the Dowager Empress you know, has tried to persuade the Tsar to banish that so-called priest Rasputin, who they say advises the Tsarina who in turn advises the Tsar – so they are saying that Rasputin is the real Emperor!" fumed Father. "And," this said with rising outrage in his voice, "the Tsar has ordered the Empress to leave the capital so she has taken up residence here in Kiev."

It was evident from all that was said that war weariness and privations were causing discontent in and around Kiev as elsewhere in the Empire. There was a growing shortage of winter fuel. Women, refugees, and prisoners of war had become the workforce in the factories that had switched to wartime manufacturing. As in Petrograd, many of the large houses had been turned into temporary hospitals. Like so many other wealthy women, Mother did what she could to assist with the Russian Red Cross and other hospital work. The Dowager Empress, Maria Feodorovna, had been president of the Red Cross and so they had spent some time together at the Mariyins'kyi Palace where the Dowager had taken up residence. The Red Cross was able to train nurses in six months. This was enough time for them to learn the technical details of nursing, but Mother felt that it was too short a time for them to learn the wider knowledge and skills that nursing required. During my all-too-brief visit home I accompanied Mother on one occasion to the Palace where these women had gathered to plan their own war campaign to try to relieve some of the suffering. The drab sepia colour of the war had transformed life even here; I could not help making the comparison with my visit just thirteen months ago.

"Thankfully, the wounded who arrive here only come for convalescence; I don't think I could bear to see what happens in the field hospitals or help on surgical wards like the brave Tsarina and the devoted Grand Duchesses," observed Mother on the way home, her voice a curious mixture of awe and deep sadness. As the coach rumbled through our estate, the faces of the peasants seemed to have changed — perhaps it was just my imagination. Father had told me that there had been difficulty getting the peasants to help with the haying this year and a great deal had been stolen in the process. People we had known for years had become surly and obstructive, demanding higher pay and compensation because of the war effort. I found myself feeling anxious for my parents and the chill I felt was more than just the effects of the first flakes of snow.

The snow fell deeply overnight, and Piotr had to use the sledge the following morning to take me back into Kiev and I walked down the hill to the railway station. The train journey back to General Headquarters at Mogilev, though only a distance of about four hundred miles following the Dnieper River, took much longer than usual. The train had to keep making stops to allow sufficient steam to build up because the quality of fuel supplies was becoming increasingly poor.

On my return to duty, I discovered that the Tsar, seemingly having lost faith in some of his staff, had ordered many of his personal officers and guards, to the front line. Nikolai Sergeyevich was given the command of a brigade on the southern border.

"So, Ivan Ivanovich, we finally have our chance to win some honours for Holy Russia. With my height I will cut them down from above, and you, my short Cossack, will dodge between their legs," he mocked.

That was the last time I saw Nikolai Sergeyevich.

CHAPTER 4

CLOSE ENCOUNTERS (1916)

It was not until the following October that I was given the command of a cavalry brigade responsible for the defence of bridges and other fortifications. In the meantime, my duties in His Majesty's Escort continued. The Imperial family were with us in Mogilev for the anniversary of the Konvoy regiment, and we officers, in full Cossack dress, posed with the royal family for the photographs taken to mark the occasion. Towards the end of the month, we travelled south to a town called Rovno, west of Kiev, where General Brusilov had his headquarters. From the station, the Tsar, the Tsarevitch who was with him, and the Suite, went by car out towards the forest, escorted overhead by a squadron of aeroplanes, to visit the troops and a military hospital. The escort followed in separate cars. In the distance we could see the long grey lines of the units massed in the forest. The Tsar and Tsarevitch walked down the front of the troops and then bestowed decorations. We then proceeded to visit the casualty station. We entered a dark forest and eventually came to a small building. The Tsar and Tsarevitch and some of the Suite entered the house while we remained outside on guard. An old woman was standing near the hospital evidently waiting for something. When the Tsar appeared, coming back out of the building, the old woman ran towards him waving something. Instantly those on duty nearest the woman barred her way. But the Tsar had noticed her and indicated that she should be allowed to approach and spoke to her.

"What do you want, old woman?" The woman was clearly overwhelmed and terrified. She fell to her knees, and without speaking handed him the letter that she had been waving. Without speaking again, the Emperor took the letter, put it in his sleeve and walked back to the waiting transport. We heard later that the woman's husband, who had been unfairly sent to Siberia, was released.

Back in Rovno, knowing that we would have at least an hour to wait for the Imperial party to depart, I took the opportunity to have a look around the town since I had never been there before. From the station I could see the domes of a church less than a mile directly in front of me, but the centre of town seemed to be to my right, and I could see at least two more churches in that direction and guessed that I might also find a few shops. I turned right and walked a short distance down a wide main road paved with stones with a footpath covered with bleached wood. I turned left, crossing an iron bridge that spanned a shallow river, made wider by marsh and swampy banks, and came to an open marketplace. Somewhere near the river's edge I could hear what sounded like a blacksmith striking his anvil and could just detect the smell of smoke from the furnace. Here, I could see evidence of fighting, scars of battle from when the German army had reached the town in the early stages of the war.

Unlike Kiev, there was very little grass and few trees in the town itself, but surprisingly, the marketplace, paved with old bricks, was bustling with people. A large horse-drawn cart rumbled by carrying a huge barrel of water; I could hear the liquid sloshing as the barrel rocked to the rhythm of the horse's movements. A group of barefooted children scampered past me as I stood and breathed in something akin to normal life.

The town had wide streets and looked as if it had been prosperous before the war; there were banks and branches of some of the big Russian commercial firms now boarded up. The population, many of whom had fled eastwards ahead of the German army, seemed preoccupied but furtive. Though Polish myself, I became acutely aware of my Russian uniform and a feeling of suspicion directed towards me. I hesitated to go further and pondered the strange futility of the situation. Here I was in Russian-occupied Poland, defending Poles from the Prussians, but serving the Russians rather than my own Polish people so that I could protect my Polish family.

As I stood there lost in thought, I became gradually aware of a farm cart trundling towards me, laden with baskets of fruit and large wooden caskets. An elderly gentleman who looked to be in his seventies, with a distinguished moustache and the proud bearing of a military man, drove the cart. Beside him sat a young woman dressed simply in a once-elegant gown that was now dusty and faded from overuse. She wore a simple peasant-like scarf over her head but sat erect and as proud as the elderly gentleman. There was something about them that seemed to hold my attention. I watched as the cart slowly drew up alongside some other farm vehicles in the marketplace and the young woman climbed down. She must have felt my gaze, because she turned and looked directly at me with an inquiring tilt of the head. Instinctively I smiled at her and received in return a broad smile that completely transformed her face; the tired eyes lit up, her white teeth flashed, her cheekbones seemed to become more pronounced, and something seemed to pierce me through the heart, causing me to gasp for breath for a fleeting moment.

Somehow, I had forgotten that I was a Cossack on duty; I only knew that it was imperative that I should speak to this young woman as if the whole of the rest of my life depended on it. She turned away to reach up to one of the baskets, but the spell was not broken. I found myself striding over to her side and lifting the basket of fruit down for her. Neither of us spoke as I continued to unload the baskets. Before lifting down the first of the caskets, I finally spoke,

"Do you want these caskets lifted down as well?"

"Yes please, but carefully; they are full of honey and quite heavy. Thank you," she replied in a husky youthful voice.

At this point, hearing voices, the elderly gentleman slewed around on his seat to see who was talking. Seeing in front of him not only a Russian soldier, but a Cossack, he pulled himself up still further, and barked out an order to the young woman as if she were a private in his regiment.

"No dawdling Sofia. Make a proper note of all transactions. Now is not the time for gossip," he said, nodding his head as if to say that I was dismissed. Instead of leaving, I found myself taking one of the young lady's hands and bowing over it as I had seen my father do with my mother so many times.

"These hands are too fine for a farmer's daughter," I said, speaking my thoughts aloud.

"They are pianists' hands," she confessed shyly, "when the war is over, I shall be a schoolteacher," she added with total confidence. Her words conjured up an image of my mother's finely tapered fingers.

"When the war is over, I shall come and find you, Sofia," I promised. I saluted the old man, turned, and strode away without looking back but felt sure that I was watched all the way until I had turned the corner to cross back over the bridge and go back to the station.

During the next few months, over Christmas and into the New Year, the visits to the front continued, to Galicia, back to Tsarskoe Selo, to Riga on the north coast, to the Crimea and the south coast, to Podolia, and back to General Head Quarters at Mogilev. When we visited the areas that bordered Prussia, we were told that the people still in that region were either spies or residents who were informers for the Germans on the Russian movements. The Russian troops in these regions experienced no special hostility; the inhabitants were indifferent to the military but happy to sell their produce to whoever would buy.

There was a lull in hostilities before the Spring campaign, but much of the population continued to flee eastward. People were frightened from their homes by battles in and around their towns and villages. We saw these people, who having loaded their household goods, children, and old people onto carts, joined the unbroken ceaseless current of people moving from west to east. The rain forced them to use the macadamized roads which then overflowed with traffic and slowed progress. Like a swarm of locusts, they destroyed the local supplies in their wake. Amongst this disorderly mass of humanity disease ran rife and the whole route of the exodus was marked by small hillocks with hastily erected crosses over them. Those who reached the railways were offered transport and town councils and the Red Cross organised feeding stations, medical help, and accommodation. This exodus of the population caused difficulties for our Russian troops, who often had to stop and fight a rear-guard action to allow the crowd to make room for the troops and their transports.

In the summer of 1916, lectures were arranged for officers at The Nicholaievsky Academy, to which those who had practical experience were sent, me included. In October, there were reverses in Romania and all available reinforcements were directed there. The Tsar had appointed General Gourko as commander of the 8th Army, based in the Volyn region of Russian-occupied Poland and that is where I was eventually sent in command of a cavalry brigade. We were based near Lutsk, and I was keenly aware that this was just thirty miles west of Rovno.

Billeted with our horses in an abandoned barn, just a few miles behind the newly dug trenches of our infantry division, I made the acquaintance of Boris Alexeevich. Unlike Nikolai Sergeyevich, Boris was quiet and serious, a philosopher of sorts, and an expert storyteller. We sat leaning against some lumpy old sacks that appeared to have a quantity of potatoes in them, already sprouting roots in the darkness and damp where they had been abandoned unwashed and smelling of earth. I noticed that Boris had several days of growth on his chin and guessed that I must look the same. There was a dark smudge at the side of his rather delicate feminine nose that seemed to draw my attention. As he spoke, he would pause periodically and twitch his nose like a rabbit and the smudge would crinkle. In my head I wanted to say, 'you have a smudge on your nose,' but I found that, as so often since I had been sent to the front, my thoughts simply stayed in my head. Boris was telling a story that he assured me was all true as he had heard it himself when the story had been told to General Gourko.

"It was General Kornilov," he began, "who came to command the twenty-fifth Army Corp; he had escaped from just over a year's captivity in Austria. I got a good look at him, he was a real Siberian Cossack, with prominent cheek bones and those piercing Asian eyes.

General Kornilov told us that he was captured by the Austro-Hungarian army in May 1915 during the retreat of the south-western army from Galicia. To secure the safe retreat of the corps, he remained with a small rear guard, but was captured. He spent a year and three months in captivity, all the while thinking about how to escape. He had to prepare his escape little by little so as not to arouse the suspicion of his captors. He would need the assistance from among the local inhabitants." Boris paused and looked across at me to be sure that I was paying attention.

"Go on," I encouraged him.

"Of course, you know the story of the Biblical King David who feigned madness before Achish the King of Gath, well Kornilov did something similar – at least that's what I thought when I heard the story. He intentionally behaved insolently and ill-mannered so that the Austrians, who kept him under strict supervision, would avoid contact with him. He pretended to be ill and was sent to a hospital. There he made a deal with a chap called Mrynyak, the assistant of a local pharmacist, who promised to help liberate him in exchange for 20,000 Korunas."

"What's that in rubles?" I interrupted.

"No idea, but I should think it must be a large sum to persuade someone to take that kind of risk," said Boris with a hint of irritation and a slight frown at the interruption. The nose twitched, the smudge crinkled, and he continued. "When everything was ready for the escape, Mrynyak secretly supplied him with papers and an Austrian uniform for a common soldier. The doctor who came to visit was treated in the same insolent way and so refused to renew his visit. Kornilov's orderly, a Russian solder, after Kornilov had stealthily left the hospital, continued to assert that the General was ill and didn't want to see anyone. As Kornilov left the hospital building, an Austrian sentry, taking him for a comrade-in-arms, asked him for a light for his cigarette as he passed, but as planned, took him for a common soldier. Still dressed as an

Austrian soldier, the General boarded a train in the direction of the Romanian frontier. But before he reached the border, he jumped off the train and continued on foot, making use of the compass and maps he had bought through Mrynyak. He knew it was essential to avoid any dangerous encounters, so he kept clear of inhabited places and had to forage for food on the land."

"He's not alone there," I interrupted unintentionally as the thought in my head was surprisingly voiced aloud. Again, the frown before Boris continued.

"On the third night he decided to risk asking some shepherds for help. He told them he was a deserter and asked how to get to the Romanian frontier whilst avoiding Austrian troops. The next day he was among Romanian friends who helped him to return to Russia." There was a silence whilst I politely waited in case there was more to follow since I genuinely did not wish to interrupt again.

"Stories like that make you wonder what you would do in the same situation. I would hope to be as courageous and as wily as a hunted wolf," I said trying to sound philosophical. But Boris had finished his story and withdrew into himself not sharing his thoughts. In the not-too-distant future I was to be thankful for having heard this story and to know that it was no disgrace to use a disguise for self-preservation and escape.

By November, the Russian position on the front was strengthened and most of the army was withdrawn to prepare for the Spring offensive in the following year. In December, the Tsar stated in a proclamation that he intended to create a free Poland from the three divided provinces. This felt to me like a ray of hope during a bleak winter. The weather was especially severe; the corn-producing provinces were unable to transport the corn to the railway stations, and those that did get through found the trains themselves snowed in. That same month we heard that Rasputin had been murdered. Boris had family in Petrograd and had received a letter that he found perplexing.

"It seems that the Marie Theatre is still open, and people are still going to see the ballet, but at the same time there have been strikes and violence in the streets," he told me in a muffled voice with his head down and his chin tucked in.

"There is anti-Tsarist feeling openly talked about in the ranks," I observed hoping that my tone of voice didn't indicate my feelings on the subject. Boris lifted his head and looked up as if staring into space, and without a single twitch of the nose and with the conviction of a preacher, made clear his own feelings.

"Whatever the defects of Tsarism may be, it is the beam that ties all Russia together. It is the basis and framework of Russian society, the sole link between all the different territories and peoples which centuries of history have gathered under the sceptre of the Romanovs. Cast away Tsarism and you'll see Russia fall apart. To whose advantage?" I had nothing to say. In the distance we could hear the rumblings of a barrage. To answer Boris, I would have to think about a future, and I could not picture anything beyond surviving the next action.

To every corps was attached a separate Cossack cavalry brigade of about two hundred men from the second reserve. My regiment consisted of three battalions. Our role was the support of communications and military administration, but much of the time we were repairing or demolishing bridges and railway lines. With the introduction of position warfare, using trenches and fixed positions, the cavalry had become an auxiliary arm to the more numerous infantry. It was not suited for defensive tasks and our horses required favourable terrain. Before an expected battle, we provided the scouts, who were the major source of information, and acted as skirmishers whose task it was to conceal and protect the main body of the army from the scouts of the enemy.

There was a time when the Cossack cavalry would charge en masse at the enemy's lines, but now we were taught to use a 'lava' formation. This was a type of loose formation charge designed to put the enemy off balance, with the attackers lapping around the edges of an enemy formation; it had a chaotic appearance but a definite purpose. Yelling and firing, we swarmed like angry wasps all around the enemy to disperse them and enable hand-to-hand combat, allowing us to bring into play our superiority in handling our weapons. We were armed with three-line five-round bolt action rifles that were shorter and lighter than the infantry equivalent. When mounted, our rifles were slung across our backs and were carried with a sword; as officers we carried a sword and a revolver. We never doubted that we could charge bravely enough when the time came and that nothing else mattered very much. We saw ourselves as part of an elite, distinguished from the common soldier because of our horses and sabres.

In 1914, at the beginning of the war, most cavalry officers were titled. But in the intervening years so many had been lost that many were raw recruits, and although fighting dismounted was only to be undertaken when mounted action was impossible, the cavalry was reduced to scouting, the occasional pursuit of the defeated enemy and to dismounted combat.

It was February and a dense leaden mist hung heavily over the leafless birch trees and marshes ahead of us. I was in command of a patrol of about thirty cavalrymen with instructions to locate the position of the enemy batteries from which there had been shelling for the last twenty-four hours. The shelling had stopped and there was a disquieting silence as we halted to listen. The ground was still frozen, so the terrain was accessible for our horses who fidgeted in the unusual stillness. There was a low ridge close by where there appeared to be fewer trees, perhaps a clearing, or farm track. I dismounted, indicating to Boris and two others to do the same, leaving our horses with the rest of the patrol. Crawling to the edge we could see what looked like an enemy patrol who appeared to be testing something like an old track possibly to see if it would take the weight of their mobile guns.

Our standing orders were to protect our army from enemy scouts, so I gave the order to prepare to attack and mounted up. With Boris at my side, we manoeuvred our horses to a position just out of sight but level with the enemy. The horses began trotting but kept increasing their pace to a gallop. I was aware of the thud of their hoofs and the jingle of weapons. Then on the word 'Charge' the horses were urged to full speed. Driving my spurs into the horse's flanks, my horse, flourishing its tail, extended its neck and galloped faster. We thundered down the track, yelling, with swords flashing before the enemy patrol knew what was happening.

The horse on my right squealed and fell as the shots began to rain down on us. But only for a moment as we made contact and guns were slashed away. Then all was confusion in hand-to-hand combat until something hit me on the head just as though I had been kicked in the head by a horse rearing up. I felt my legs buckle and was aware of the pain as I fell forwards wondering why my arms hung limply by my side but was unconscious before I hit the ground.

CHAPTER 5

REVOLUTION AND ESCAPE (1917)

I was taken to the Lazaret field hospital but have little recollection of the journey; much of the time I was thankfully unconscious. What became of Boris and the others I never found out. The hospital seemed to be near to the front which I couldn't understand. The first night I was woken by loud reports and suddenly the earth shook to the accompaniment of a terrific crash like the sound of a collapsing building; the crumbling of stone and the shattering of glass and metal. I remember lying there in horrible anticipation of the next jolt that I felt sure would come. Unable to defend myself – or anyone else – I felt utterly helpless. The guns roared all night long and through the open doors I could see flashes from the exploding shells and the whole visible sky was aglow. The sound of guns became a continuous roar of thunder in my head and when the shells landed, I could feel the shock through the earth and everything in the temporary ward rattled.

A hospital orderly, a sanitor, had dressed the wound on my head, giving it as her opinion that I had been struck by a sword. As I lay there in the semi-dark, I became aware of a nurse watching me. She was dressed in the typical Red Cross uniform worn by the Sisters of Mercy, with white overalls over a grey linen dress, but in addition she wore a leather jacket to keep warm. She looked to be in her forties and somehow had a motherly look about her. She noticed that I was looking at her and came closer, smiling. She spoke to me, but I found myself feeling confused, I wondered if I might be delirious or had received some kind of brain injury. She must have noticed my confusion because when she spoke again, I could understand her although she spoke in stilting and very poorly pronounced Russian.

"I am English," she said, pointing to herself she added, "my name is Sister Isabella."

I found myself reaching out my hand, and she, trying not to slip in the mud, took my hand between her two hands in a firm clasp. Her hands were cold, and her genteel fingers were swollen with chilblains from constant contact with cold water. A shell burst nearby, and the shock seemed to travel from the ground right through her causing her hand to tremble. I let go of her and put my hand up to my head running my hand over where I had been bandaged. The tight starched bandage covered my ears and seemed to have been wrapped under my chin. I wanted to speak but my voice seemed to belong to someone else; I could hear the rasping sound coming from my throat. Sister Isabella bent her head to listen, and I tried again,

"I understand English," I said, "You make me think of my mother," I said, closing my eyes and summoning up the image of my mother dressed in her straw-coloured gown in the blue supper room with the sun streaming through the window. Sister Isabella smiled and drifted away to watch over the other patients, many of whom were moaning or coughing. An orderly came and helped me to drink some unknown liquid and I fell into a fitful sleep.

Some days later, a young soldier a few beds away, who had not long undergone some sort of surgery, began to call out for water. His desperate cries became an unceasing torment to all of us other patients; I couldn't understand why no one would give him any water. I could see that Sister Isabella was upset and having some sort of inner debate with herself. There was a mug of water standing near one of the other men. The young soldier had seen it, and raising an arm pointed to it. His face was fiercely alight with his need to assuage his thirst. After an inward struggle, Sister Isabell picked up the mug and held it to his lips. The soldier, crazy with thirst, seized the mug, and tilted it upwards. The water splashed into his open mouth and over his face and pillow as he swallowed in noisy gulps and then lay back on the pillow in relief. But then, to my horror, there came a strange gurgling sound and out of his mouth poured a stream of thick greenish fluid that spread over his bed and dripped to the floor; he stopped breathing. Sister Isabella was distraught; it was a few days before she was back on duty.

As further casualties arrived at the field hospital, those who needed convalescence were transported to the cities, to the hospitals that had been set up for this purpose. I was taken in a red cross truck to the nearest railway station and transferred to a hospital carriage where we lay in bunks for the journey. Our destination was Petrograd, but the journey was a long one. Reserve troops, munitions, and supplies had to take priority and we made numerous stops. We were told that there would be a lot of hold ups because of exceptionally heavy snow fall and a shortage of labour to clear the tracks.

As we travelled further from the areas of military action, there seemed to be an increasing confusion of orders and conflicting messages about where our destination should be. Several times the train was stopped and boarded, and searched by police; I had no idea what they might be looking for. Eventually arriving at Petrograd, we were taken by Red Cross truck the short distance from the station to the hospital. As we were stretchered out of the truck, I looked up at the familiar building of the Sergei Palace, residence of the Grand Duke Dmitri Pavlovitch on the Nevsky Avenue next to the Fontanka River, with its distinctive orange façade.

"This is the Anglo-Russian hospital; the Dmitri Hospital," said the driver pointing to a flagpole on the roof where a Union Jack fluttered in the chilly breeze. We were taken in, through the Concert Hall where the beds were all occupied, and into one of two rooms that opened onto the Concert Hall. How it had changed! There were two rows of hospital beds at each side facing each other. The parquet floors had been covered with linoleum, the damask and engraved plaster walls had been covered with plywood; only the chandeliers were visible high up in the lofty rooms, and unlike the field hospital, light streamed in through the windows that went up to the ceiling.

I was taken to a bed against a wall where part of the plasterwork was just visible above the plywood covering. There was a plaque on the wall; I guessed it was written in English but could not see it from my lowly position. As a count, the son of a count, I had received the best education and spoke Polish and Russian, and had learned German, French, and English. This was important as the Imperial family spoke to each other in English. At the earliest opportunity I asked one of the English nurses to tell me what the plaque was.

"It is to commemorate the individual or British town that has provided money for the hospital," I was told, "this one says Newcastle-on-Tyne." I often wondered about the people of Newcastle-on-Tyne during my stay in the Dmitri hospital.

Our beds were made by the ward maids, the 'sedeilka', and our wounds were daily dressed by the 'sanitors', but the English nurses in the hospital kept us entertained. The English nurse in command of the hospital was Lady Sybil Grey, daughter of an English earl. She had a natural air of authority but carried it with grace and humour. I remember noticing how her curly hair escaped defiantly from whatever head covering she wore giving her a girlish appearance. Her face was longish, in the English way, and she had an aristocratic nose, but her eyes were soft, gentle, and intelligent. Her lips were full, but when she needed to be forceful or summon up strength, she pursed her mouth into a thin line. Even then a kindly smile lurked in her eyes. She had a small scar on her cheek where she had been injured by a grenade whilst visiting one of the field hospitals.

"You probably won't believe it," said Sister Mary – one of the younger nurses, "but when that dreadful Rasputin was murdered in December, it was the owner of this Palace that did it, him and Prince Yusupov."

"Yes, we did hear about it; I was at General Head Quarters with the Tsar at the time," I agreed.

"Ah but what you won't know," continued Sister Mary in hushed tones, "is that they came here and took refuge in the Duke's private apartments. The police came looking for them and they would have been arrested and executed if found. The Duke gave Lady Sybil a great big iron key to the only way into his apartments and she kept it hidden under her dress for three weeks!" she said dramatically and taking a breath before continuing. "And the Prince got a fish bone lodged in his throat and Lady Sybil, calm as you like, arranged for it to be removed." Sister Mary lifted a finger at me to stop me from interrupting, took a few more deep breaths and then finished with a flourish. "And while she was sheltering those men, some of the Mad Monk's supporters, seeking revenge on the Grand Duke, invaded the hospital. Lady Sybil, cool as a cucumber, faced them without flinching and saw them off the premises. Now, what do you think of that?" she said with satisfaction as she watched my face, standing with her sleeves rolled up above the elbow and arms akimbo. She had portrayed the picture so graphically I burst out laughing and felt much better – and so did Sister Mary. It wasn't long before I would see Lady Sybil in action for myself.

It was March and I was enjoying my convalescence in this Anglo-Russian hospital. My wound was healing nicely, there was no sign of infection or any secondary or internal injuries. I was allowed to eat in the patient's dining room opposite the main staircase, beyond the dressing room. There had been a lot of talk of shortages of bread and wood. In the newspapers we read that there was a transport crisis and the extreme cold, which had all Russia in its grip, had put more than a thousand engines out of action due to their boiler tubes bursting. The snowfall in the last few weeks had been exceptionally heavy. When Sister Mary walked by, she seemed agitated and anxious, she kept rolling her sleeves up then pulling them down again in an unconscious repetitive move. I called her over.

"You seem troubled Sister," I began, "is there something wrong? Can you tell me?" Still fidgeting with her sleeves, she replied with a nervous laugh.

"Oh, I expect I am just being silly, but as we walked past the bakery this morning on the way here, it seemed to me that their faces, I mean the poor folk who were lined up in a queue, most of whom have probably spent the whole night there in the freezing cold, well their faces seemed to have a sinister expression. I felt frightened of them, but I don't know why." She shook her head, finally decided on rolling the sleeves up, and walked briskly away.

In the afternoon we could hear people shouting outside. Some of the nurses went to the windows watching the people queuing for bread in the freezing temperatures. Some of the women were shouting "Bread and peace!" People had begun gathering outside on the Nevsky Avenue and the surrounding streets. Those of us who were mobile joined the nurses at the window. Judging by their clothes, it looked as if the women had been joined by striking mill hands and munitions workers. There was a small commotion near the entrance to the hospital as a small platoon of soldiers from the Volhynian Regiment of Guards arrived. They had been sent to guard the hospital, and we realised that whatever was happening in Petrograd was not just a simple disturbance.

About five o'clock in the evening, Lady Sybil arrived on the scene with her cool, determined manner. She calmly walked to the window, and standing quite close to me, watched the unfolding events. We could hear the crowd chanting: "Down with the government; down with Protopopov – the Minister of the Interior; down with the war; down with Germany." We watched as Cossacks arrived, clearly sent to quell the crowd. Shots were fired, but the crowd was undeterred and began throwing stones at the troops. In response, the soldiers lay down in the snow and began to fire a volley into the crowd. I heard Lady Sybil gasp, and then rap out a sharp order as if she were in the military.

"Ladies! Prepare the theatre for surgery immediately! There will be casualties." She went herself to summon the surgeon and prepare to assist. There were casualties, and six of them died, two of them were women, no doubt someone's mother; three civilians and three policemen dead and at least a hundred wounded. This wasn't war, and somehow these deaths, of unarmed civilians, seemed more tragic to me than much of what I had seen in battle. The injured were still in surgery or having wounds dressed when there was yet another commotion as the threatening mob surged into the building wanting to search it. Lady Sybil stood her ground and sent them out, but clearly did not trust the soldiers to keep the hospital safe. She had the foresight to issue instructions for red cross flags to be made using sheets and a red St Nicholas suit – she called him Father Christmas. These were to be strung across the balcony to show the mob that this was a hospital. We could hear parades and processions continuing until late, the crowd singing the 'Working Man's Marseillaise'.

In the evening, the nurses were escorted to their sleeping quarters across the street during a lull in the fighting. But I doubt if they slept well, the streets were alive with gunshots, screams and shouting. The police headquarters next to the nurses' home was broken into and we heard that many of the policemen had been murdered.

The next day, we heard that the Military Governor of Petrograd had put up placards all over the city. According to this declaration, all meetings or gatherings were forbidden, and the civilian population was warned that the troops had permission to use their arms to stop at nothing to maintain order. Looking out of the window, we could see that this warning had made no difference. The mob in the Nevsky Prospekt was still increasing. We watched helplessly as troops fired on the crowds; there were scores of dead civilians. I was uncertain as how to respond. Officially I was still on sick leave, but my former regiment, the Cossacks of the Escort were here in Petrograd, and I toyed with the idea of re-joining them. As it turned out it was fortunate that I hesitated in my decision.

Early the next morning, we heard strange noises coming from the east of the city. We learned later that a disorderly mob carrying red flags had crossed the Alexander Bridge from the right bank of the Neva River. The Volhynian Regiment that went to meet it from this side, had mutinied during the night. It was rumoured that they had killed all their officers and had joined the parade coming towards us up the Nevsky Avenue, calling on other troops to join them. I realised, with a rush of adrenalin, that if the rumours were true, I was suddenly in a very vulnerable position. A couple of hours later we heard a burst of firing and from the hospital we could see flames somewhere on the Liteyniy Avenue. From our vantage point we could see frightened inhabitants scattering through the streets. On the corner of the Nevsky and Liteynyiv Avenues, soldiers and civilians seemed to be erecting a barricade and we could see flames from the Law Courts. Soldiers still loyal to the government took up positions opposite the barricade and the sound of machine gun fire could be heard. I wondered where the machine guns could have come from. One of the other patients, who was evidently more familiar with Petrograd, seemed to have read my thoughts.

"The revolutionaries must have got into the Arsenal," he said dispassionately, "it's on the Liteynyiv."

As the day wore on, we could see that more buildings were being set alight; they were all government buildings. We heard later that the buildings that were in flames included police stations and that the prisons had been opened and all the prisoners had been liberated. The Fortress of St Peter and St Paul was under siege and the Winter Palace had been occupied; there was fighting in every part of the city. That night only the most heavily sedated of the patients had any sleep, the rest of us lay in restless helplessness while the night nurses huddled together in corners whispering. The firing died down overnight but never ceased.

The noise of fighting close by began again the next morning. Armoured cars could be seen with machine guns, displaying red flags, passing by and over the bridge at top speed. We could see that new fires were blazing at various places across the city. The troops appeared to have fallen into anarchy, with no leader in control, spreading terror throughout the city. I had only one thought by this time, to get home to my family estate. I had no idea what was happening at the front with the war effort, where my brigade would be, or even where His Imperial Majesty was in all this. There was still too much confusion and street fighting for me to risk the short distance to the station yet, I would wait a few more days. Lady Sybil's red cross flags seemed to be working, there had been no further invasions of the hospital, so I felt safe where I was for the time being.

On the following day I began to wish I had set off sooner, although whether the trains would have been running is doubtful. In the papers was an announcement known as Army Order No 1. This order instructed soldiers and sailors to obey their officers and the Provisional Government only if their orders did not contradict the decrees of the Petrograd Soviet. It called on military units to elect representatives to the Soviet and for each unit to elect a committee to run the unit. All weapons were to be handed over to these committees and were not to be issued to officers. There was a report that leaders of the Provisional Government had gone to the Volhynsky barracks and made fiery speeches in which they told the soldiers, who had already killed their officers, that if they remained loyal to their oath to the Tsar they would be subject to the death penalty but if they joined the revolution, they would have immunity. As a result, the Regiment, without the officers, put themselves under the orders of the people.

The parades that day were more orderly; there were a few officers wearing either a large red cockade in their caps or a knot of red ribbons on their shoulders and red stripes on their sleeves. I was stunned to see that the Cossacks of the Escort, the Regiment of His Majesty, His Majesty's Railway Regiment and the Police of the Imperial Palaces had joined them. News of the Tsar's abdication came the next day. For me this was the deciding moment; I had to return to my family estate. I waited one more day to see if things would settle but instead new demonstrations were beginning, this time against the war. By now the revolutionaries were in control of the railways, and anyone connected with the Tsarist regime was being rounded up and arrested. In all parts of the city revolutionaries were ruthlessly tracking down so-called traitors, police, and government officials who had served the Tsar.

The weather was very dismal the next day; from dark and heavy clouds dense snow was slowly falling in large flakes. From the hospital window the snow was so thick it was impossible to see even the railing on the bridge over the Fontanka River. I decided that the weather would give me my best chance of escaping Petrograd. I dressed in my uniform – the only clothes I had, and furtively took the thin blanket from my bed to wrap around my shoulders like a cloak; my own cloak was probably still at the field hospital. Thankfully, the few roubles I had were still deep in a pocket; there should be enough to pay for passage on a train and to pay any bribes that might be needed. The less anyone knew about me the better and so I left without a word to anyone.

The snow was already deep and still falling, slow and thick, and would cover my footprints within minutes. Despite the weather, there seemed to be large numbers of disinterested soldiers milling around aimlessly, and most of them appeared to be drunk – so much the better for me. I pulled the blanket closer around me, hoping to cover most of my uniform and trudged on over the bridge and along the Nevsky Avenue to the railway station. My objective was to get to Kiev with all possible speed, but in the first instance it was a priority just to get out of Petrograd in one piece.

Inside the palatial building, there were few civilians, and the soldiers here were clearly in control and well ordered. The most direct route in normal times would be south via Gatchina; the route I had taken so many times to General Head Quarters at Mogilev. But with all the confusion surrounding the Tsar and the difficulties with supplies to the front, it seemed to me that it would likely be safer to go first to Moscow where, as far as I knew, the revolutionaries had not yet taken complete control. Having become familiar with the train routes, I knew which line to aim for and noticed that there was a train that appeared to be heading in the right direction. I discarded the blanket and hoped that if I simply walked confidently to the train, as if I had every right to travel, that no one would notice. I was wrong.

I was arrested before I reached the first carriage. My uniform betrayed my rank. Several soldiers barred my way; their rifles raised with me in their sights.

"All officers are to be arrested, your Excellency," said one of the soldiers who was immediately reprimanded by one of the others.

"There are no more Excellencies in the Soviet, Comrade," he shouted angrily, "All officers should be shot!" he added with venom. I thought of my mother and pictured her face as I wondered if this was indeed the end for me.

"Take him to the Commissar for interrogation," said another voice that appeared to decide the matter and I was marched to a room that might have been a waiting room at one time but had been occupied by some sort of militia and set up as an interrogation room. I had no idea what sort of information they hoped to get from me. The Commissar, an undistinguished looking man seemed to be reading some sort of bulletin and was clearly not enjoying what he read. He looked up with an expression of annoyance as we entered.

"An officer for interrogation, your Exc... er Sir; we arrested him trying to board a train to Moscow," said the soldier. The Commissar's expression of annoyance was replaced by one of tedium.

"And what am I to interrogate him about?" he asked, but it was clearly a rhetorical question and the soldier wisely kept silent. "Yes, yes, I shall deal with him," he said nodding a dismissal. The soldiers, trained to salute, but no longer expected to, shuffled out in some disorder; if I had not been in fear of my life, I would have found it comical. The Commissar began by asking my rank etc and asking why I was in Petrograd and why I was trying to get to Moscow. I explained that I had no interest in the revolution. I told him that I was Polish and simply wished to return home to my family. The Commissar then indicated that I should go with him and then led me into a smaller inner room. Would this be where I was to be tortured, I wondered; I couldn't understand what they hoped to find out from me. But the room was almost bare; there was just an old wooden bench pushed up against one of the walls and a pile of old tickets that seemed to have been stored there for some time. The Commissar shut the door and then turned to me with eyes alight with intrigue.

"Listen," he said in conspiratorial tones, "I am Polish too; I am also looking for a way to escape from this hell hole. I will help you escape, but it will not be easy. If you are caught you will be shot, do you understand?"

"I understand your words," I said, "but I do not understand why."

"Why does not matter right now," he said and went on, "these revolutionaries are mad with their new-found power. Anyone who has served the Tsar, even in a minor way, or has had any kind of privileged life is a target for these insurgents. You will only survive if we can disguise your rank and status. This will take time, maybe a week; are you prepared to do this?" I thought of General Kornilov who had spent more than a year planning his escape and a disguise; a week seemed very short a time by comparison.

"I have no choice; if you are prepared to help me, I will follow your lead," I said, the relief that came with his words finally beginning to take effect.

As it turned out, the Commissar kept me 'detained' in that room for just five days. He found civilian clothes for me to wear, including coarse linen underwear and a pair of very old shoes. He gave me no washing facilities or razor for shaving, and I was expected to slop out a bucket each day. He gave me work oiling various pieces of machinery. I slept on the floor and was given very little food; I was genuinely hungry. There were moments when I wondered if this was all part of some horrible new means of preparing me for interrogation and at the end of the week the real interrogation would begin.

"The revolutionaries always look at a person's hands," said the Commissar, "if their hands are clean, smooth and soft, they will recognise that you are not from the working class. You must not shave, and you must keep your hands dirty and oily. They will even check your underwear, believe me, you will have to wear these."

After five days, my skin was itching, my eyes were red and swollen from the fumes, the lack of fresh air, and lack of sleep, and my face was pinched with hunger – this part of my disguise was not fake. The Polish Commissar arrived with a loaf of dark bread and a bottle of Vodka for my journey, and I stuffed them deep into my pockets with grateful thanks.

"You had better go tonight," he said quietly, "there is to be a funeral tomorrow, for those who have lost their lives, in the Field of Mars. There may be thousands of people in the streets; it will be a good distraction, no one will notice that you have gone."

For a final touch, the Commissar handed me a stick so that I could walk with a limp. I put my remaining roubles into various parts of my clothing and hoped that during any searches they would not be discovered, at least until I had reached home.

"Remember that your educated speech will give you away," warned the Commissar, "avoid speaking if you can and if you have to, well try to sound like a peasant," he added with a wry smile that told me that he didn't think I stood much of a chance.

Waiting for dark, and an opportune moment, the Commissar marched me onto the platform and threw me unceremoniously into the cattle truck of a train that I vehemently hoped would be going to Moscow and not to Siberia.

CHAPTER 6

RETURN TO KIEV (1917)

It seemed to me that the train remained in the station at least two hours; I was already stiff and cold before we eventually shunted slowly away, heading for the south. I had taken a few tiny sips of the Vodka, hoping to make it last all the way. Sitting in the dark, the words of the Polish Commissar came back to me, reminding me that my speech would give me away. I tried to speak like one of the moujiks – the peasants, using their incorrect grammar and slurred pronunciation. It sounded ridiculously unconvincing, and I began to laugh. The laughter unleashed a torrent of emotion and I found myself weeping silently at my change in circumstances and for the terrible tragedy unfolding around me. In the calm following this outburst, my head began to clear, and I tried to formulate a plan.

I was about to take a small sip of the Vodka when an idea occurred to me. If instead of drinking the Vodka I poured it deliberately over my clothing, so that I would reek of alcohol, I could slur and muffle my speech by pretending to be drunk. A drunken peasant would hardly stand out in the crowd.

"What about something to drink?" I reasoned with myself, "I should be able to refill the bottle with water at the next station," came my answer. At that time, it was the rule that stations had to provide free clean water for passengers just as residents of Petrograd had to provide clean fresh water for people who passed by their houses. I hoped that this rule had not yet been abandoned. I set about pouring the Vodka carefully over my outer clothing in such a way that it would create the most odour but without soaking through and making me wet. At the earliest opportunity, I supposed the first station that we came to, I planned to leave the cattle truck, fill the bottle with water, and get into a proper carriage with other passengers. If I got thrown off for not having papers, it would be because the authorities would think me a drunken peasant rather than a fleeing officer, formerly of the Tsar's Own Escort.

When the train shuddered to its first stop, I waited for the sound of some activity to be sure that it was a station and then clambered out. Sure enough, there was water available – hot water for making tea, but it would cool down soon enough. I managed to wrap part of my coat around the bottle so that it wouldn't scald me. Then limping with my stick and swaying slightly to suggest intoxication, I went towards the first passenger carriage, and without checking as to its class, climbed in, and sat on the first available seat.

In the dim light of the carriage, I could see that I had unintentionally climbed into a first-class car. Looking around, I could see a distinguished-looking elderly gentleman gently dozing at the other end. I supposed that at the next station I might be able to switch carriages if I had not already been thrown off by then. In the meantime, I sipped the hot water and nibbled on the loaf of bread. The soporific effect of the warmth, combined with the gentle rocking rhythm of the train, put me into the deep slumber of exhaustion.

I was woken abruptly by the sound of slamming doors and the uncouth voices of soldiers shouting and joking with each other. I forced myself awake and tried to recall where I was and what was my situation. By the time I had reassembled my thoughts it was too late to try to change carriages; instead, I decided that I should appear to be still asleep. The elderly gentleman was clearly not amused by the invasion of armed soldiers.

"What," he demanded in an imperious tone, "are you doing in a first-class car?"

"There's no more first class anything," shouted one of the soldiers.

"We're going home," stated another, "back to our families and our villages where we belong." The elderly man persisted,

"Do you soldiers have leave of absence?" he demanded.

"No," was the general reply.

"We are going; just so," stated a particularly deep-voiced soldier with an air of finality.

"And when will you be returning to your regiments?" continued the elderly gentleman, clearly not able to let the matter go.

"The war might be over before we have to return," came the reply, this time from a younger voice that exuded passion and a supressed energy. "We soldiers are represented now, in the Council of Workingmen's Delegates, we are allowed to retain our rifles, and we can vote," added the young voice to rousing cheers. The elderly gentleman was unable to say anymore as the soldiers broke into song, "O rise, working people, to the factory let's go..."

It seemed to me that my safest course now would be to stay put and keep my head down. So long as the soldiers did not suspect me of being an officer from the Imperial army, their presence would effectively allow me to remain where I was. This proved to be the case since passengers at subsequent stations, on seeing the soldiers, avoided our carriage. Not wanting to risk leaving the train until we had reached Moscow, I kept my sips of water to a minimum and nibbled the bread only to stave off immediate pangs of hunger.

After many hours I began to recognise some of the surrounding countryside north of Moscow through which I had travelled by train before. How different was this journey from the journey with the Imperial family just three years earlier; how different would the arrival in Moscow be.

The train finally pulled in at the Nikolaevsky station. I waited until the soldiers and the elderly man had left the carriage before picking up my stick and reminding myself to limp. Looking along the platform, I could see that a group of men that looked to be some kind of militia were stopping people and asking questions. As I limped and swayed in their direction, hoping not to be noticed, one of the group swaggered up to me and demanded to know where I was going and what right I had to travel on the train. I mumbled and slurred some nonsense under my breath and drooped my eyelids, keeping my eyes fixed on the floor and using the stick to steady myself. He came close enough to smell the alcohol and took a step back but as he did so, he snatched at my free hand and proceeded to inspect it. Evidently, it was dirty enough to satisfy the fellow. He threw my arm aside and waved me away, growling at me to get out of the way. By this time his attention had been transferred to a commotion surrounding the elderly man who seemed to be someone of importance. I made good my escape.

The Nikolaevsky station is on the northern outskirts of Moscow, but to get to Kiev I had to cross the city and make my way towards the Moskva River where the Bryansk Station was being rebuilt. The most direct route would be right through the centre and past the Kremlin. I hadn't seen a newspaper in more than a week, and so had no idea how the revolution might have been unfolding here in Moscow. The streets, although not crowded, seemed orderly. The trams were running, as were the cabbies, the zimniki, and I even saw a few automobiles with red flags flying on the main avenues. But there was clearly a shortage of supplies here in Moscow as there had been in Petrograd. Long bread queues stretched for blocks along many of the streets. The expression on people's faces told me that they had been waiting for a long time and there was a now familiar undercurrent of unrest. Signs outside the shops such as 'price depending on availability' told their own story.

As I passed the Kremlin, I could clearly see evidence of fighting. There was damage on the walls from what looked like artillery fire. The gates of the Nikolskaya Tower were hanging askew on their hinges and much of the brickwork had been blasted away. As I headed for the bridge, I suddenly heard shots being fired somewhere behind me. Trying to maintain my limping cover, I hurried into a side street, hoping to avoid involvement in whatever was happening. An automobile filled with armed militia sped past and shortly afterwards crossfire and shouting could be heard. I decided to take a more circuitous route to the station, avoiding the main roads. The effect of the false limp was starting to take its toll and my hip really had begun to cause me pain, and by this time I had run out of water and only had about a quarter of my loaf remaining.

I hobbled across the bridge over the Moskva River and looked up at the newly completed neo-classic Bryansk station with its huge glass circular structure and its high clock tower. I had no idea what, if any, trains would be operating in the direction of Kiev and what kind of restrictions there would be; I had no papers, and soldiers and militiamen were swarming around the station seemingly ill-disciplined and leaderless. I hoped I had sufficient roubles to pay, or bribe, my passage on a train.

As I drew nearer, one giant soldier stood in my path, his face dark and sullen with suspicion.

"Where do you think you are going?" he growled. "He looks like one of those looters to me," he said addressing his comrades. About seven or maybe eight of these revolutionary soldiers moved slowly closer, staring, and beginning to mutter, "Looter." I heard someone else say, "Thief." The giant soldier suddenly swung his rifle off his shoulder and pointed the bayonet straight at my heart, growling "Search the thief." The mass of people began to close in like a pack of hungry wolves. Two strong arms grabbed me from behind and several men began rifling through my pockets at the same time. One immediately found the remains of my loaf.

"Bread!" He shouted, "There is no bread to be had in Moscow; he must have stolen it." This was followed by calls for me to be arrested. Another man found a few roubles in another pocket and waved these about, shouting, "Look; this drunk must have stolen this money." All this time I kept hold of my stick and managed to keep up the pretence of intoxication. The man who had found the money must have presumed that since he found no more in any of my coat pockets, that there was no more to be found and released me so that he could count his haul. At this point a fierce argument arose as to what was to become of the spoils. The giant solder, aware of his size and strength, snatched the bread for himself and proceeded to eat it, thus creating a general uproar that gave me the opportunity to surreptitiously melt into the crowd.

Once safely inside the station, I decided to abandon the stick as the limp that it had induced was causing too much pain. The smell of the alcohol was wearing off, but I felt that the effect of not having washed or shaved in such a long time would be sufficient to avert suspicion. I took out the roubles from one of my hiding places and with it was able to bribe my way onto a train heading in the right direction.

"You won't get far on the train," I was warned, "the bridges have all been destroyed." Of course, that was only to be expected, I had destroyed enough bridges myself to understand the methods of war and I was heading towards the Front. My meagre collection of roubles was dwindling, but enabled me to travel, changing from passenger trains to hospital trains, to military trains, and peasant carts, eventually arriving with nothing in my pockets in Kiev.

The city was crowded with war-weary peasants in soldier's uniforms who had returned from the front. There seemed to be some sort of demonstration going on near Khresshotyk Street. Curiosity drove me closer; I heard the crowd shouting and saw the banners proclaiming, 'Long Live a free Ukraine'. Clearly Ukrainian independence was a driving force amongst revolutionaries in this region and I wondered what this would mean for the mainly Polish landowners, such as my own family and friends, west of the Dnieper River.

The poplar and chestnut trees still lined the boulevards in the city, and I thought of the steep slopes of the Imperial Gardens on top of which stood the bronze statue of St Vladimir with a solemnly raised cross. Mother loved to walk in the gardens at this time of year as there would be a wonderful view of the spreading Dnieper River. Water would flood the low-lying land on the opposite bank, deep into Chernigov Province, almost to the horizon. It seemed then that Kiev was standing by the seashore.

Heading towards the main road leading to our family estate, it seemed to me that Bolshevik 'Red Guards' were already forming here in Kiev. I resumed my limp and shuffled past these groups of men, keeping my eyes down and hoped not to attract any attention. If they had checked my hands they would have been satisfied with their filthy appearance and if they had searched me, they would have found nothing to benefit them or betray me, but there was a slim risk that this close to home someone might recognise me despite the growth of facial hair. They were engrossed in fierce political debate and, apart from one or two cursory glances, I was ignored.

Before leaving the station, I had the foresight to refill my bottle with water, for which I was very grateful knowing the long walk I had ahead of me. The thought of good food when I reached home sustained me on what I presumed was the last leg of my journey. The trees were just beginning to come into leaf and turning a bright fresh green, but there was still a chill wind, and I was not going to reach home before dark. There were several small villages that I would be passing through and I wondered if I might be able find shelter in an outbuilding overnight – a thing I had become used to before I was hospitalised. The small, steep-roofed thatched log cabins in the villages seemed as war weary as the people and many were in desperate need of repair. The few peasants that I encountered had a dejected appearance and at the same time their eyes held a mixture of malice and apprehension. Fearful of being recognised, I kept my head down and shuffled past.

The long straight earth roads were damp and muddy, but the grass verges were soft to walk on. When it was too dark to see my way, I searched for a suitable outbuilding and found a dilapidated and abandoned old stone barn. The roof had long since disappeared, but at least there would be shelter from the wind. It would only be for a few hours; I planned to set off again at dawn, knowing that I had not far to go the next day.

I was wakened by a light drizzle about an hour or so before the sun came up. In the grey half-light, I could see something moving like ants on a higher patch of open land. Trying to make sense of what I was looking at, my anxious brain morphed them into a surging crowd of people; a search party looking for someone to arrest. The sun nudged its way over the horizon and flooded the landscape with colour. The ants transformed into a large pack of wolves. They were busily devouring their prey and so long as I was moving away from them, I should have nothing to fear. I forced myself to my feet and resumed my journey.

A few versts from home, I unexpectedly caught sight of Sowiński sitting on an old farm cart behind a very ancient horse, just turning into the lane that led to the cottage Father had given him ready for his retirement. I hailed him and strode up to the cart very glad to see the familiar old face and hopeful of a lift the rest of the way home. I did wonder, somewhere at the back of my mind, why he was driving this old cart rather than being driven in one of the carriages. He pulled on the reins inexpertly, and the poor horse, unsure what it was supposed to be doing, snorted and tossed its head. Sowiński turned stiffly to look behind him, a look of consternation on his face.

"Your Excellency!" He breathed. "Come, you must not be seen here. Quick! Get up into the back and cover yourself with some straw, then lie down and pretend to be asleep."

"No Excellencies allowed anymore; haven't you heard?" I asked laughingly.

"Hush!" he hissed, "You are not safe; I will take you back to my cottage; you must not be recognised; we are both in danger now." He was clearly very frightened, so I obeyed without any further conversation. Climbing onto the back of the cart, I lay down and pulled a few handfuls of straw over my clothing, shut my eyes and pretended to be asleep. The cart rattled and bumped along in the stillness for about twenty minutes and then pulled up. Not knowing if we had reached our destination, I stayed lying down with eyes shut until I felt Sowiński pulling at my trousers and indicating that I shouldn't speak. Some peasant women, carrying bundles of clothes for washing in the river, were just a stone's throw away. We slipped unseen and unheard into Sowiński's small wooden cottage.

The cottage was a typical one-room thatched-roof cabin made from logs from the forest. The logs had been cut to give a flat edge on three sides so that they could be stacked more easily and create a smooth inside wall.

Between the logs there was mortar and moss to keep out the wind and the rain. A large wood-fired stove stood at one side with an L-shaped chimney that vented through the wall. A wooden floor had been boarded over the dirt but looked as if water would come up through if there was a heavy downpour. It was very simply furnished; there was a table and a stool and one high-backed chair into which I slumped. Sowiński indicated once again that I should not speak and went to listen at the door. Only when he was absolutely satisfied that no one was within earshot did he speak. He perched on one of the stools, covered his face in his hands and between stifled sobs told me that my parents were dead.

"Oh, Janusz, my boy, it was terrible... terrible... I saw it all... but what could I do? I couldn't help... I would have died with them but they wanted someone to be here for you when you returned... they believed you would..." Sowiński was trembling and tears rolled down his distraught wrinkled old face at the memory.

"But how are they dead?" I asked mystified, "What did you see?" Perhaps I shouldn't have asked but sometimes we need to know what happened to our loved ones no matter how horrendous that knowledge might be.

"They were murdered. Some of the men who did this were your own peasants, but they were stirred up to it by some rebels who came from other villages; I have never seen them before. They told your workers that the government in Kiev had said that all land and property belonging to the Church, or the State or noble landowners was to be redistributed." Sowiński stopped speaking as he buried his face in his hands once more. Then in a muffled voice and without lifting his face he said, "They tortured your Mamusia and Tatus and then hung them up by the legs."

I had been on the battlefield, and I had been wounded, I understood about suffering, but this; torturing and murdering innocent people, this I did not understand. As I empathised with the sufferings of my parents a wave of nausea washed over me; the shock-induced vomiting lasted about an hour before my exhausted body finally let go of the inner tension and I wept.

Poor Sowiński, pale and drawn, who seemed to have aged even beyond his many natural years, pottered around on unsteady feet, trying to find some means of offering comfort. He fed and watered me, sharing his meagre rations. As the hours passed, I began to feel a rage and anger, but the reality of the situation came home to me, and this was replaced with fear as my survival instinct kicked in. I suddenly stood up with renewed energy and asked Sowiński to help me one last time before I left my home estate and escaped to the west.

"I need your help, old friend, to get me into the house. I will need some of my plain civilian clothes – I can't go on pretending to be a peasant, my speech will give me away, but if dressed simply I could be a clerk or accountant or some such thing. There are also one or two things in the house that I would like to take with me if they haven't already been looted." I said with a resigned determination.

Under cover of dark, Sowiński took me on foot using a cross-country route to the back of the house. There was just enough moonlight to see our way, but I was glad of Sowiński's lead; I would have had to follow the road and risked being seen. He led me to one of the servants' entrances and took out a large iron key to unlock the plain wooden door. We entered what I presumed was a scullery and then proceeded along a dark passageway, stumbling over objects that were strewn over the floor.

"Clothes first," I whispered and was led towards the great hall from which I knew my way. This part of the house was completely denuded of furniture, and I began to wonder if I would find any clothing in my rooms. Some of the portraits and paintings that lined the walls on the grand stairway had survived, but others had been maliciously destroyed for no purpose. I deliberately avoided going into any of my parents' rooms; I could not bear to carry the recollection of destruction with me into the future, only the happiest of memories. In my rooms, again most of the furniture had been looted, and much of my clothing had been scattered about and probably discarded as impractical for labouring wear. I was able to change into some clean clothes and was especially glad to change my undergarments. Sowiński stood anxiously watching me, wringing his hands, and pleading with me to hurry.

"You don't understand, your Excellency, there are gangs of murdering bandits roaming the countryside; please hurry."

"Yes, you're right; I need a bag for some supplies, my father's revolver, and ammunition, and then I must go down into the basement. Father doesn't... didn't trust banks; he kept a store of gold hidden in the cellars; I only hope it hasn't been discovered." I told him as I rummaged through the piles of my belongings strewn around the room, hunting for an appropriate bag.

The store of gold, cleverly hidden behind some brickwork, was untouched. I gave some to Sowiński, telling him to bury it when he reached home and only use it in an emergency; if it became known that he had gold it could be a death warrant. I put as much as I could reasonable carry hidden in torn compartments of the bag, inside the lining of my long coat and anywhere else that it could be hidden about my person. We left the house in silence. I did not look back. Sowiński led me again to his cottage where he gave me what food and drink he could spare. He wept soundlessly as we embraced and I had gone before the sun had risen; I strode away, heading west through the forests.

CHAPTER 7

THE POLISH ARMY (1918)

With a vague idea of looking for some remnant of the family, I planned to head towards the town of Zaslov on the River Horyn where my cousin Joseph and his family had a comfortable estate. As far as I knew we were still at war with Germany, and I had no real idea what I might be heading towards. I reckoned that the journey to Zaslov would be about two hundred versts and I anticipated taking between ten days and two weeks to get there, assuming that I was not held up for any reason.

Zaslov was almost directly due west from Kiev, and by not allowing myself to drift south, I could keep to wooded and forest areas and avoid large populations. My route was crossed in many places by streams, lakes, and minor rivers, so water was never a problem. I divided my supplies into fourteen daily rations, in the expectation of being able to eat properly when I arrived at my cousin's home. But the nights in April are still bitterly cold when you are tired, hungry, and have no real shelter. Most nights I broke off small branches, roughly criss-crossing them to try to weave them into some sort of windbreak. The younger branches would have been bendy enough to weave but they were also too green to break off. There were a few abandoned cottages or barns that I was able to shelter in or by, but since I was trying to avoid contact with people, I kept mostly to the denser woodland.

My thoughts kept returning to my parents and their ghastly death. As far as I knew they had always been kind, fair, and generous to their tenants, especially to the elderly who could no longer work. They were certainly generous to Sowiński who loved our family as his own. I could not recollect any occasion when my father had spoken disparagingly of any group of people, although he would not tolerate idleness or dishonesty. My father had always been fiercely Polish, and it had been a struggle for him to watch me go to serve in the Russian Imperial Army but had reconciled it with his conscience knowing that I would be helping to defend both rich and poor alike against an invading enemy. These same poor folk, whom I had been fighting to defend, had murdered my beloved parents. I certainly had no sympathy with those who sought to overturn society to satisfy their own desires; it seemed to me that envy and malice was the driving motivation for the violence and destruction that I had witnessed.

I continued to travel west until I reached the River Horyn. From there it was a short distance south to Zaslaw. At a small cottage on the edge of my cousin's family estate, I decided to call in to enquire about the family before venturing up to the house. To my great astonishment, Joseph himself opened the door and stood looking unrecognising at me, with a sullen and suspicious expression in his eyes, and a slight glance past my head as if scanning to see if I was alone.

"It's Janusz," I said quietly in response to his evident fear, "your cousin Janusz... from Kiev," I added. His eyes widened slightly in surprise, but he gave no other sign of having understood me, but with a shrug of annoyance he opened the door wider, indicating that I should go in.

Although we were cousins, there was little family resemblance; I had inherited my stature from my father, but my colouring and features from my mother. Joseph had inherited the features of the Russian side of his family; there was even a hint of red in his hair. Still without speaking, he motioned to a large wooden table and chairs at one side of the room. It was near enough to the oven in the centre of the room to feel the heat but far enough away not to be uncomfortable. Following his example, I sat down in silence, swinging my bag to the floor at my feet. I then watched as he poured hot water into a large brass samovar and felt myself relax as it began its familiar whisper, sizzle, fume, and steam. He then made tea for us both and sat down in silence, periodically glancing at me under his brows. I took a breath as if to speak and he indicated that I should remain silent. We sipped our tea, me grateful for a hot drink in a warm room, him shifting his eyes from side to side as if listening intently. After several minutes he got up and casually closed the wooden shutters at the window. Then at last he spoke.

"Jan, it is good to see you. Do not speak until you have heard what I have to say; there are spies everywhere; it is close to anarchy in the region. You are not safe here; officers of the Tsar's army are being arrested, and property is being confiscated from all the landowners and redistributed. The revolutionaries have already set up a Council of Workmen and Soldiers in the town. My family fled east in the autumn two years ago ahead of the German advance. At the time I was on the Northern Front. They left the estate abandoned; I can only hope they arrived safely as I have had no word from them." He paused for a long moment, staring unseeing into his cup; clearly there was another picture in his mind. I waited while he sipped his tea and then he resumed. "After Order Number One was decreed by the Petrograd Soviet, which, as you know, effectively instructed soldiers to disobey and disarm their officers, and dispense with military discipline. Like you, I discarded my officer's uniform, and came here to await events. In time I plan to re-join the army perhaps in the lower ranks, help fight the Germans, and hopefully regain a command once things have settled down. You can stay here for a while if we can keep your identity hidden; if arrested, former Imperial officers are being deported to Siberia... or executed." He stopped suddenly and seemed to expect me to show some surprise.

"I have already been arrested once, and escaped," I told him. "When I returned to Kiev, I found my parents had already been murdered by the revolutionaries; I cannot go home. What happens to me now will no doubt be determined by the outcome of this war." I paused and re-ran in my mind some of the events of the last few weeks. "I would not wish to re-join the Russian army even if they would tolerate it; I do not see that life for the poorest peasant is any better in the hands of these revolutionaries." I paused again, realising that I had been expressing my unguarded thoughts aloud, and instead tried to find out how the local Council Joseph had spoken of was working. He seemed pleased to be able to demonstrate his knowledge of how affairs were unfolding in the town. He poured more tea and carved a few thick slices of dark bread, which I gratefully received, before settling into a long discourse on events. I was in no hurry; I had plenty of time on my hands.

Joseph told me that the new Council took place in the town theatre where the meetings were attended by several hundred people. It was presided over by an insignificant puffed-up local official, of unknown nationality, who called himself a Social Revolutionary and had been selected as a representative to the Petrograd Soviet. According to Joseph, everyone wanted to make a speech at these meetings. They nearly all wore red ribbons or some sort of red token to show that they were supporters of the revolutionaries. At one of the meetings the soldiers had requested the right to choose their own commander just as the Petrograd soldiers had been told to do and had made it clear that they didn't care if the Provisional Government in Petrograd said it wasn't lawful for them. He had read reports in the newspapers that although the Provisional Government in Petrograd were continuing with the war, some units, and even whole divisions, were refusing to follow the orders of their commanders. He particularly wanted me to know that at one of the gatherings held in the theatre there was a meeting of Polish delegates who had made proposals for the re-establishing of a free and independent Poland.

"I have heard rumours of a free Polish Army being planned in France," he said, watching me closely for a reaction, "but I can't see what they hope to achieve from there," he added with a slight inflection at the end as if asking a question. Still exhausted from my two-week trek and feeling somewhat unsure of my cousin, I said nothing. I chewed on my bread, sipped my tea, and tried to comprehend all that was happening. Only a few months ago I had been with the Emperor at General Headquarters and knew that a summer offensive on the Western Front had been planned. But now I had no idea if, or by whom, this would be carried out. If discipline in the army was collapsing as Joseph had said, the Western Front would fall, and the whole region would be occupied once again by the German army.

"If the Russian army is defeated, we may find ourselves living under a German government of occupation, and the plans of these revolutionaries will come to nothing," I replied, evading the Polish independence question.

Within a few weeks, the German army had advanced through Galicia and reached the Zbruch River, just a day's drive away by motor car. The Russian summer offensive had collapsed before the Austrian troops, and as predicted, we found ourselves under German occupation. A group of German staff officers was billeted in Joseph's family home, and since the Front was now east of Kiev, they treated the local population, if not with courtesy, with indifference. The Polish forces serving under the then Minister of War for the Regency Kingdom of Poland, Josef Pilsudski, had been working with the Central Powers against the occupying Imperial Russian army, but in July, we heard that Pilsudski had forbidden Polish soldiers from swearing an oath of allegiance to the Central Powers. He was arrested and imprisoned in Magdeburg in Germany, and his Polish units were disbanded.

The war was still raging in the west, but for us the summer and early autumn months were about survival on the land, helping peasants in the fields and orchards, avoiding officials of all types, and keeping a very low profile. My gold was well concealed; I did not even let Joseph know of it. In October, we heard of further trouble brewing in Petrograd. The Provisional Government was overthrown by the Petrograd Soviet. For us, still under German occupation, it had little effect at first. The 'scorched-earth' policy of the retreating Russian army in 1915 had already ravaged the region, destroying, and burning property and crops, plundering the homes of the local population who were forcibly evacuated east, and blowing up bridges, mills, and railroads. Now, under German occupation, the peasantry found themselves being taxed on what little food they had and the grain that they did produce was being requisitioned for the German and Austrian troops spread across the occupied territories. We weathered the winter and wondered what the new year would bring.

Despite the German censorship of newspapers, we heard reports that a formerly Russian-Polish corps of soldiers in the north had refused the orders of the newly established Petrograd Soviet to disband and had instead joined the German army against the Red Army of the Bolsheviks. It was difficult to really know what was happening, or who was in charge, except that the German military presence did offer a harsh stability.

"And the Ukrainians in Kiev are once again demanding their independence," said Joseph, "they're just causing more trouble. This land has been Russian for so long, the

Russian people, whether revolutionaries or imperialists, won't just give it up," he added almost fiercely and gave me a challenging look. I had little desire to enter into debate but felt compelled to speak.

"From what we are hearing out of Kiev, it sounds as if the Russian soviets are trying to restore the old Imperialist order, crushing any hopes of independence from Russian domination," I muttered angrily.

"All these people who want independence, how can it work when all these different people with their different languages have been living all mixed up together for so long. How can you separate them? It's not possible. I have heard that in Kiev, if you are heard speaking Ukrainian, or wear an embroidered shirt, or even a grey cap, you might be shot," said Joseph disbelievingly. "We had better stick to speaking Russian; we may be occupied by Germans, but we are surrounded by peasants who seem to think that the Bolsheviks will give them a share in the land," he added derisorily.

"Before this war everyone seemed content to live alongside their neighbour whatever language they spoke, or so it seemed to me." I said, speaking more to myself than Joseph. "I know our peasants were well taken care of and we all just learned everyone else's language, Polish, Russian, German, French, and we read their literature and enjoyed each other's music and poetry. Perhaps all this envy and malice were there, but we didn't see it," I said somewhat naively I thought afterwards, "but a desire for independence from an Imperial or colonising power I can understand," I added, aware of my own father's passionate hope for a free Poland.

In March we heard that the Petrograd Soviet had made a deal with Germany at a town called Brest-Litovsk. The Germans were now able to occupy the region unhindered and began to move further east towards the Crimea. The occupying authorities became more extreme in their repression. We guessed that this was because the German army was now spread so thinly across former Russian territory and of course were still entrenched on their Western Front. The local population were told that for every German soldier killed or wounded, the authorities would seize and shoot ten of the local inhabitants, and they ordered the death penalty for any disruption to the food supply.

In April we heard that the Germans had set up a puppet government in Kiev; in command was a former general of the Imperial Russian army. There were riots, uprisings, and social unrest that were brutally supressed. We continued to keep a low profile and thankfully no one gave us away. Of course, I was unknown in the locality, but Joseph might easily have been recognised. In May we heard that the Polish corps, that had been working with the German army against the Bolshevik army, had been forced to disband. But we also heard that the core of the military personnel had moved into Polish territory, west of the Bug River. I decided that the time had come for me to move on and perhaps join the remaining Polish army in Warsaw. Joseph remonstrated with me, arguing that I would be safer staying with him; that anything could happen to me travelling alone.

"If the Germans catch you, they'll probably think you're a spy; if the Ukrainian nationalists catch you, they'll target you for being Polish," he said with genuine concern.

"True," I admitted, "not even the local Germans are safe; I heard from one of the peasants that some German farmers, that have lived here since the time of Catherine the Great, have been targeted by Nestor Makhno's anarchists. But I have no real ties here — other than yourself of course, and I feel sure that my father would have wanted me to play my part in any future free and independent Poland."

I persuaded Joseph to let me have an old farm cart from one of his family's abandoned barns and we managed to find a broken-down old donkey to pull the cart which I loaded with what I hoped would be enough supplies to get me to the Polish capital. We found some old clothes and I hoped that I would look like just another displaced refugee, which of course is what I had somehow become. Following the flat open country of the wide Horyn River plain, the old donkey got me as far as Rovno; from there I planned to travel by train to Warsaw.

Having followed the river, through birch and oak forests, I managed to cross the bridge at Hoshcha and followed the steep road down into the town, past the old prison standing by an old grove of trees. Already on this journey I had encountered other refugees travelling towards Rovno, and as I slowly drove down the long straight main street, I found I was not alone; I had joined the stream of displaced persons in the westward flow of the current.

Under the relative stability of the German occupation, the town was bustling with people; the narrow alleys leading off from the main street were crowded and muddy. I was aiming for the marketplace, hoping to sell the donkey and cart, making a mental note to repay Joseph one day for his kindness. I guess there were shortages of carts and even broken-down old donkeys because it took very little time for them to be sold.

As I approached the station, the smell of coal from the locomotives filled the air, accompanied by whistles and bell ringing. I had no clear idea where, or to whom I should go to enlist in the Polish Army and began to wonder if I had made the right decision. Almost at that moment, I caught sight of a familiar face. There was no mistaking those black dense eyebrows creating a ferocious expression. I was sure it was General Yuri Danilov, known at headquarters as 'Danilov the Black'. He was neatly dressed in civilian clothes but carried himself with military precision. Knowing my own unkempt state, I hesitated to make myself known and involuntarily stepped back out of his way as if to salute. This movement drew his attention and he looked directly at me without any recognition. When he had been stationed in Kiev, my father had known him well; it seemed probable that like me he was now no longer serving in a Russian army. Apologising for my appearance, I introduced myself, telling him briefly of the fate of my parents.

"Ivan Ivanovich!" he had exclaimed, using my Russian name that seemed to belong to a dim and distant past. "Are you here for anything in particular or just passing through?" he barked as if asking for the dispatches of the day.

"I have no fixed plan," I admitted, "although I was planning to go to Warsaw."

"You look half-starved and in need of a shave," he said bluntly, "You will come and be a guest of my family while you think about a fixed plan," he said echoing my words and compelling me in the direction that he was taking. "I have retired from the army you know. I have had a house here in Rovno since 1906 when I was first stationed here in command of the 166th Infantry Regiment," he explained. "So far the Prussians and Austrians have left us in peace; they are too busy trying to quell the uprisings all the way to the Black Sea. My guess is that the war on the Western Front will soon be over and then we'll see what they'll do," he added. I followed meekly, allowing him to expound his views on the progress of the war on all fronts; the treachery of the Petrograd Soviet in suing for peace with the Central Powers; and his prophecies for the future of his beloved Russia, until we arrived at his large, old, three-storey comfortable house on the west of town near the railway that had somehow survived the ravages of war so far.

Sitting in his tastefully furnished drawing room, sipping hot tea, the General began to reminisce. I listened politely and joined in when I could, trying to remember all the various personalities with whom I had just a distant acquaintance. He interrupted himself, and fixing me with those ferocious black eyes, said abruptly,

"No point going to Warsaw." I waited expectantly for him to continue, with slightly raised eyebrows. After a long pause, in which his eyes wandered around the room as if searching for a thought that had drifted out of reach, he continued.

"The Polish Russian corps went over to the Prussians to help stop these accursed revolutionaries," he began. "Now the Prussians have made a deal with the Bolshevik devils and disbanded the Polish corps. Your General Pilsudski is languishing in a German prison. What good would it do to go to Warsaw now?" It was clearly a rhetorical question, so I waited for him to continue. "You are most welcome to stay here with us until..." The General seemed unclear how to continue and with genuine gratitude I thanked him for the offer, and it was settled that I should stay with them until I had made other plans.

I spent the next few months enjoying the hospitality of the General and his family. During the day I wandered through the town, getting to know some of the smaller alleys, avoiding the occasional gathering of nationalists or other activists, and watching as commerce and trade began to resume. Most days I went into the market hoping for a glimpse of Sofia and her image continued to play on my mind. In the evenings the General wanted to talk; he had reached that stage in life when everything that had happened in his youth had become rosy and everything was better in the old days. I rarely saw his sons, just occasionally at mealtimes, and never discovered what they did all day.

In the November of '18, everything changed. The Central Powers, defeated on the Western Front, capitulated, and signed an Armistice. The agreement effectively annulled the Treaty of Brest-Litovsk opening wide the question of

Russian borders. General Pilsudski was released from Magdeburg Prison and the Polish Regent Council appointed him Commander-in-Chief of the Polish Forces. Poland proclaimed their independence. At the same time, there was revolution in Berlin and the German forces began a steady withdrawal from the eastern territories. Into the power vacuum spilled the Red Army. To make matters worse, bands of Ukrainian nationalists began threatening towns, targeting Polish landowners and former officers of the Russian Imperial army. General Danilov wasted no time.

"My friend, Ivan Ivanovich, I and my family will be leaving this house as soon as I can make the arrangements. I shall sell this property and all its furnishings, and we shall emigrate to Paris, France. You may stay until then, but I would advise you to leave also; you were both a Polish landowner and a former officer in His Majesty's Own Escort; they will hunt you down if they find out." The General's voice trembled with emotion as he spoke, but he gave out his marching orders as if he had been on the field; there was no sign of fear for himself, only concern for his family.

"If you will permit me, and if I have the correct sum, I would like to purchase your house," I said, and by way of explanation added, "I have my reasons for wanting to keep contact with this town. I plan to offer my services to General Pilsudski to fight for a free Poland as I know my father would have wanted. I will keep your house servants on to manage and maintain the property until I can return." The General was stunned but recovered himself quickly as he realised the benefit this would mean to him and his family. They would be able to leave as soon as they had packed their most precious items with which they could easily travel.

The transaction was carried out remarkably quickly as I was able to pay in cash with my father's gold. The Danilov family were gone within a few days. I settled the retainer fees and obligations with the house servants and set out myself for the railway station. As I passed the marketplace I searched again in vain for a glimpse of Sofia and then headed to the imposing two-story blocks of the railway station. I was filled with a strange sensation, not a longing for the past, but a sense of loss, as I approached the building where just two years ago, I had been part of the grand Imperial procession. Now my destination was Warsaw, my objective the Polish Army.

CHAPTER 8

IN THE SERVICE OF THE MARSHAL (1919)

Everywhere along the route into Warsaw there were signs of the ruin that had been wrought by the intense fighting of the first year of the war. The roofless houses, factories with only a solitary chimney to show where they had once stood, old trenches, and humped graves told their own tragic horror stories. In Warsaw itself, now in the grip of winter, the children on the streets were without shoes, their feet wrapped in rags. The people seemed to have barely enough clothing and showed all the signs of having been insufficiently fed for many months. The hollow-eyed listless children did not even have the energy to play. Their weak little bodies were just bones clothed with skin but no muscles; some couldn't walk, and they simply couldn't play. The bread, which I tasted on first arrival, seemed to have been made from herbs and moss, and tasted horrible. Added to their physical discomfort, the population must have been suffering mental distress caused by the conflicts of the past and the ongoing military unrest that seemed to surround us all, casting a haunted expression on many faces.

Having declared independence, Poland now seemed to be fighting on all fronts, against Germans, Czechs, Ukrainians, and Russians. General Pilsudski had been trying to organise, in addition to his core troops, a Citizen's Guard, and a volunteer militia. But there were shortages of equipment, munitions, uniforms, and even shoes. The hospitals had few if any supplies, and the air was filled constantly with rumours and reports of revolution, conspiracies, corruption, and treason as conditions grew steadily worse. This was the Warsaw in which I arrived, and such was the army in which I enlisted. As an ex-officer from the Tsar's Imperial Guard, I was immediately given a command with the rank of Major.

Beyond Warsaw, the conditions for the population, as the post-war turmoil continued, worsened by the day. We heard reports that in some towns and cities such as Vilna and Lvov, people were beginning to die of starvation. There must have been similar suffering all over Europe after the devastation of the previous four years.

We heard reports that in the wake of the retreating German army there was increasing anarchy and the further east you went, the worse the anarchy. Armed paramilitary groups, operating under flags of different shades and hue, emerged in many localities, such as black anarchists, green farming populists, white monarchists, red Bolsheviks, and blue and yellow Ukrainian nationalists. In January, there was great excitement in the capital when the world-renowned pianist, Ignacy Padarewski, was declared Polish Prime Minister. I witnessed his arrival in Warsaw where he was met by vast cheering crowds. The peasants took away the horses from his carriage and then pulled the carriage themselves all the way to the Hotel Bristol. The streets were lined with cheering masses all the way. I wondered if these crowds would be as fickle as other similar cheering crowds I had witnessed over the last few years.

Padarewski, aware of the vulnerability of the newly independent republic, feared a Bolshevik invasion and this fear was largely justified. Moving rapidly, they had already reached the town of Biabstok, just northwest of Rovno, by March. In his speeches, the Prime Minister warned of torture and murder, and what he called 'the menace of barbarism'. The Polish Army responded. We reoccupied much of the territory over the next few months, despite the intrigues of the Soviet secret police who had entered Poland in the guise of the Russian Red Cross, trying to stir up revolutionary fervour.

But it was not all war for us. In August, we received a visit from Herbert Hoover, who had been appointed by the American President Woodrow Wilson to lead the American Relief Administration that had already begun to send food aid, clothing and even shoes for the children. At the train station, the Mayor of Warsaw presented Hoover with the traditional welcoming gift of a large round loaf of bread with salt crystals on top. This was a ceremony that I had witnessed numerous times whilst in the service of the Tsar. I don't think the Americans quite knew what to do. The hosts had placed the loaf on a large and heavy wooden platter. Because Hoover was already holding his hat in his right hand, he tried to hold the platter in his left hand, but it was too heavy. We then witnessed the amusing spectacle of him handing the platter to the admiral that was standing next to him who likewise passed it on to the next person, and so on all down the line to great applause by those watching. All the while military bands kept up a continuous stream of music, alternating between Polish and American anthems. Once again, I found myself witnessing vast crowds paying homage to one man. The primary schools had organised the children of Warsaw to take the day off school. Tens of thousands of children walked barefoot in a parade for the American philanthropist, many of them waving American flags.

The next day there was an open-air Mass in Saski Square. Later, we all went back to the Belvedere Palace where a photographer arranged us on the terrace for the official photographs to be taken. Hoover, the Prime Minister, General Pilsudski and several other dignitaries were seated. A few officers were made to sit in front and the rest of us stood behind while the comical long-haired photographer hopped about trying to coax us into position, taking twenty or thirty pictures. Again, I had a feeling of 'deja-vu' as I posed for a photograph with internationally renowned dignitaries and the equivalent of Polish royalty.

Children seemed to swarm wherever Hoover went. In the Hotel Bristol, they had strewn flowers all up the marble steps making them dangerously slippery. There certainly didn't seem to be any shortage of flowers in Poland at that time. On the following day we all assembled in the grandstand of the Warsaw Horse Racing Track at the Mokotow Field. Children from all over Poland had gathered in a grand parade to say thank you to the 'Food Tsar'. There were probably about fifty thousand children. The procession lasted all afternoon and into the evening. The field in front of the grandstand was packed with people including small children. The cheers roared repeatedly. The place was filled with a cacophony of bands all playing at once as they marched past. I found myself laughing at these miniature soldiers marching like veterans. A steady stream of individual children or small groups were brought up to Hoover to give him a bouquet or some other flower arrangement, like tribute for Caesar, that banked up around him. His eyes were red, and I am quite sure there were tears in his eyes, as there were in the eyes of others who witnessed this event. The head of the French Military Mission to Poland, General Paul Henrys, with tears running down his cheeks, leaned over to Hoover saying,

"There has never been a review of honour in all history that I would prefer for myself to that which has been given you today."

Many of the children were carrying tin cups and pannikins from which they had just had their special meal served at noon in all the schools. Some were carrying little paper napkins stamped with the American flag that they waved over their heads. I can still picture the moment when the steady stream of children was suddenly interrupted by an astonished rabbit that leaped out and began to run along the racetrack. What seemed like thousands of children broke rank and rushed madly after the poor creature, shouting, and laughing; their teachers desperately trying to get them back into some sort of order. They somehow managed to catch the terrified rabbit and brought it in triumph as a gift for their hero; the great man cried. It was only a short stay and then Hoover and his entourage were gone; the conflicts surrounding us, temporarily forgotten, crowded back in.

By the end of the year, the Polish forces had advanced east even as far as Rovno, where Pilsudski ordered a halt. The General, unlike others I had known before, tended to be very private, happy with his own company, and content to make his own decisions. But on occasion he expressed himself publicly. One such occasion was when we had pushed the Red Army back out of Vilno, his native city, uncharacteristically making a speech to his staff.

"I did not expect so warm and touching a welcome. It surpassed anything I could have imagined; the people wept for joy," he said in a self-congratulatory tone, perhaps forgetting those inhabitants who had considered themselves to have benefitted under Bolshevik rule.

In December there was a temporary cessation of hostilities. The Soviet regime in Petrograd had agreed to recognise the territories currently under Polish military control and jurisdiction in return for Polish neutrality in the Russian civil war. Under cover of diplomacy, and a hard winter, the General, distrusting the Bolsheviks, planned for a summer offensive. Pilsudski's hope was that having expelled the Red Army he would be able to forge a federation with an independent Ukraine.

I took the opportunity to visit my newly-purchased home in Rovno to check that all was in order, that the servants had enough funds, and to complete any paperwork or pay bills. The family that I had left in charge of the house were of mixed Ukrainian and Polish extraction and all spoke both languages, swapping between apparently at random. As soon as I arrived, I could sense a tension in the house. Conversation was all in whispers, and when I spoke in a normal speaking voice, they jumped and jittered and looked as if they would hush me if they could. I stayed a few nights, sleeping in one of the smaller rooms towards the back of the house. During the last night I was woken in the early hours by shouts and cries somewhere in the town. The doors and shutters in the house stayed firmly locked and nobody moved, although I felt sure that others must have heard the cries. The next morning, I sought an explanation from Stanislaw.

"It's the Ukrainian army; they have a regular Hetmanate army stationed here in Rovno. It's mostly the Jews they're targeting. You can't help them; they just shoot anyone who tries to help. It's terrible, terrible. We don't know if they will come looking for Poles next. There's no one to stop them; they do what they like," he said shaking his head despondently. "Some of the peasants have tried to form a self-defence force to protect themselves and their land. They call themselves 'Greens'," he said with a mirthless laugh. "Who are they going to fight? No one knows who the enemy is anymore; everyone kills without mercy, for what?" He shrugged his sagging shoulders, cleared away the remains of my breakfast and left me to my own thoughts, shaking his head as he went and muttering unintelligibly under his breath.

I knew that Pilsudski had needed a Ukrainian ally and had made a deal with Hetman Petliura, the former puppet of the German army. Between them they expected the Ukrainian people to join the anti-Soviet cause and rally to their support to gain Ukrainian independence. I wondered fleetingly if Pilsudski knew what kind of behaviour was permitted in Petliura's army but acknowledged that there were doubtless criminals with equally vile behaviour in our own army. Such was the reality of war. I went in search of Stanislaw and found him in the kitchen with his wife. She was pouring warm water into a honey jar so as not to waste a drop of the valuable sweet stuff.

"You're right to lock the doors and shutters and stay safe. Where possible, use double locks, and keep the lights off. Go to bed early if you have to; the slightest flicker or glow will show that there are people inside, and if you have any treasures bury them," I told them earnestly, adding "and pray, as will I." I did look back at the house when I left, determined to return when all this - whatever it was - was over.

In March, Josef Pilsudski announced that he was now to be called Marshal of Poland, and in April we began our offensive against the Red Army, pushing east via Rovno, with Kiev in our sights. We had reached Rovno remarkably easily, the Marshal was confident of success. Keeping my thoughts to myself, I had my doubts. Knowing how the Russian army had so often before lured the enemy into its territory and lulled an invader into a false sense of security, I was sceptical of his confidence.

"The whole Bolshevik Army will be crushed," he had boasted, "I have made prisoners of nearly half their forces and taken materials and munitions from their base. The remainder of their army will be demoralised and dispersed. My own loss has been extraordinarily small," he continued unabashed. There was no answer or reply to his statement; I was certainly not in any position to express my doubts, rather I deliberately set them aside in the face of his confidence.

The Red Army evacuated Kiev and we entered the undefended city at the beginning of May. Our Polish forces were now occupying almost all the territory up to the Dnieper River, and, as I was acutely aware, spread very thinly along a wide front. It seemed to me that the local population, rather than rallying to our support, were indifferent to our presence. They certainly didn't sign up to fight against the Red Army as the Marshal and the Hetman had hoped.

It soon became obvious that the Red Army, just as had our army, had spent the last few months in mock diplomacy, all the while planning their next offensive. The push back came just a week later. A young captain brought me a copy of a Bolshevik propaganda leaflet that appealed to the people of Kiev to rise up and defend Soviet Ukraine, claiming that Polish landlords wanted to enslave Ukrainian workers and peasants. I took it to the Marshal who had remained deeply suspicious of Soviet diplomacy. He barely looked at it, screwing it up and tossing it away.

"Lenin betrays his Marxist roots if he now uses his Red Army to try to take revolution to Poland by force. The Polish people will not become revolutionaries at the point of a bayonet; they have no stomach for Bolshevism," he growled with contempt.

But it soon became clear that Pilsudski had overestimated the strength of our Polish armed forces, and misinterpreted Ukrainian support for Petliura and the Polish offensive. As the pre-planned Russian offensive unfolded, he acknowledged that we would have to retreat, but still hoped that an independent Ukrainian republic could be formed.

"Polish troops will remain in the Ukraine only until such time as it is necessary for a legitimate Ukrainian government to be formed," he announced boldly, "the Polish troops will retire, having fulfilled their glorious duty as liberators of the people," he continued.

By June we had evacuated Kiev, after destroying the bridges across the Dnieper River, and a chaotic retreat ensued. At the same time that the Red Army was launching its counterattack, revolutionary councils were being established in towns and cities across the region breathing vile propaganda. They blamed Polish landowners for food shortages, announcing that they were to be evicted from their estates, arrested, and deported to concentration camps. Soviet aeroplanes were used to drop and scatter this propaganda to remote and outlying districts, adding to the chaos, distrust, and violent hatred.

At the beginning of July, we had crossed the Horyn River and were back at Rovno to evacuate the troops by train. It was here that the Russian Cavalry Army caught up with us. Red-faced and bellowing, General Raszewski yelled at no one in particular.

"The enemy are encircling the city from the west! We are under attack from all sides."

When we came to the long main street in the city centre, there was a column of marching Polish soldiers, heading in the direction of the station. General Raszewski, seething with rage shouted,

"What is Berbecki doing? Is he going to march his division out of the city without any order to do so? And without reporting to me? And leave the Rovno garrison and me, its commander, to its fate?" He turned to me and spoke with surprising calm,

"Major, will you convey the order for immediate evacuation of the garrison and commence the defence of the railway station as a rear-guard action and retreat. We must restore some order to this confusion without delay."

I tried not to look around me as I headed towards the garrison; I did not want to see anyone I might recognise or be seen by them; I could not afford to feel anything. I duly carried out the General's commission and then began to make my way once again towards the station. By this time, the confusion seemed to have intensified. There were infantrymen in helmets of various shapes and colours. They were running, carrying machine guns, telephones, and exchanges. Horse-drawn wagons dashed past at a gallop. Horse riders were passing everyone, raining clouds of dust from the dry July earth, covering everything. Only the wounded trudged slowly on, wrapped in bloody bandages.

Suddenly, a heavy shell whistled overhead, forcing riders to lie flat on the necks of their horses. The ground in front of a wagon passing just a few yards in front of me, hit by the shell, rose up like a giant fountain. The wagon, that had been travelling quickly, overturned, falling into the crater left by the shell. The soldier driving the wagon was thrown out and the contents of the wagon, including what looked like boxes of munitions, buried him. I ran to his aid and began lifting the crates and boxes away. His face emerged from the jumble just as a soldier, riding a two-wheeled carriage with a machine gun covered in a white tarpaulin and carrying a scythe on his shoulder, drove by.

"The chariot of death has come for me!" gasped the dazed terror-struck soldier at my feet.

"On your feet soldier!" I said trying to keep the sound of amusement from my voice, "Your time is not yet up." His name was Stanislaw; together we made it safely to the slow-moving train headed west. The train kept stopping, sometimes for hours, and during one of these stops three soldiers came aboard; they were also returning from Kiev. They were emaciated and miserable without shoes, and, so they told us, without underwear, dragging their injured feet with difficulty.

"Where is the rest of your regiment?" I asked, fearing the reply.

"On the retreat from Kiev our regiment was encircled by the Bolsheviks in the forests of Volyn," explained one of the men who looked as if he might have been a junior officer. "We were routed and crushed. But then the Ukrainian peasants, who I thought we were supposed to be gloriously liberating, set fire to the forest to try to finish us off. We three somehow managed to get away and just kept walking until we came to the railway."

We returned to Warsaw just as the Red Army reached the Bug River. On the streets of the capital, we watched as volunteers, who had come out to defend their homeland, marched past in tight ranks for two hours. It seemed as if the whole country had formed into columns. Pupils, students, workers, and peasants, women, and men, paraded in front of their leader, the Marshal. But the speed of the Red Army advance had left our forces reeling and unprotected. Reports began to arrive from towns in the north that had fallen under enemy occupation, where the local population who offered resistance were being executed, and then Provincial Polish Revolutionary Committees were set up.

Within a couple of weeks, I was back in the field, this time trying to halt the Bolshevik advance north of Bialystok. The August rains had begun, and we were holed up in tents in a small village, with the rain constantly pounding the roof. Some of the local women risked their lives to bring us some hot food under cover of dark. One elderly woman, as she handed me some hot soup, peered into my face with hawk-like furious eyes, and gave me strict orders to rid their village of the evil invaders.

"Those Bolshevik devils are taking hostages from all the villages. And they are giving orders for more food even when there is none. Then if they don't get it the hostages are shot. Some of the people have been tortured and there have been so many arrests..." she began to choke on her emotions and the fierce look in her eye gave way to fear.

Moments later we were given the order to prepare for retreat and our tents were packed away. But the order to move didn't come and we ended up staying the night without our tents. The rain was pouring down furiously. We were soaked to the skin, standing knee-deep in mud. Suddenly the order came through and we were on the move; the enemy had reached the village. Our shoes, that had become completely sodden, disintegrated and we were forced to take them off.

The retreat continued. Populations were fleeing ahead of the invading army. In the towns the streets were choked with loaded carts and carriages. In one town, cows, oxen, and sheep were thrashing around in the streets, exhausted animals dying in the heat of the traffic jam. The people were strangely silent, but understandably determined to flee.

On my return to Warsaw, I found the streets filled with enthusiastic volunteers determined to defend their city, but the Marshal, utterly despondent had withdrawn into himself. Then just when all seemed lost, the miracle happened. Captain Kowalewski, the head of the Cipher Section burst in on the assembled staff and our great leader Marshal Pilsudski, who had all but given up on saving Warsaw. He was waving a piece of paper and shouted in great excitement.

"We've done it!" Faced by blank looks all around, he began to explain, tripping over his words in his rush to convey the good news.

"We intercepted a coded telegram. It has taken us less than an hour to decipher the main points. Listen, the order is to cross the Vistula with the 27th Rifle Division." The captain stopped and waited for a response. The Marshal rose to his feet and drew himself up, his former gloom completely vanished. We held our breath, while he cogitated and then finally gave out the order.

"We need to delay them two days to give us time to manoeuvre into a new position. It must seem to the enemy as if our forces have disintegrated, putting up no serious resistance. We will surprise them on their left flank." His tone and manner had completely changed; the great leader was back.

"I know how we can delay them," ventured the captain. "We can jam the transmission; our signals intelligence know the frequencies and call signals of all the Bolshevik stations by heart." He added.

"Won't they get suspicious?" someone asked.

"Not if we allow them to call each other, establish a connection, and then as soon as they start transmitting, our broadcasting stations start jamming by using the same frequencies," the captain explained confidently. "We will broadcast passages from the Bible."

The Marshal's plan worked to perfection; the Red Army fled in disarray in all directions from Warsaw or surrendered en masse. Warsaw was saved but we still needed to drive the Bolsheviks out of Polish territory.

At the end of August, I found myself under siege in a small town about a hundred and fifty versts west of Rovno. Suddenly, out of the dense darkness, we heard rifle fire close to the northern side of the town. Bullets rained down on our battery; shards of splintered material and shrapnel flew overhead. Then from the rear we were being pounded by machine guns. With our ammunition all but gone, the order was given to put on bayonets. The Bolsheviks lit up the battlefield with flares. In the glow, we could see our troops, the police, and local civilians, building a barricade in the street behind us and covering windows with mattresses. But after a few hours, instead of the anticipated attack, the guns fell silent. Periodically a few bullets whistled overhead and there were occasional shells exploding. Then someone was pointing to the sky.

"Those look like our boys circling up there," came an excited disembodied voice from somewhere behind the barricades. Looking up we watched as the Bolshevik artillery began firing incessantly at the tiny planes. The whole sky seemed covered with wisps of black smoke where the shells burst. Someone came running up with a handful of leaflets.

"The aeroplanes are dropping these leaflets," he shouted above the infernal din. The message was simple; we were asked to hold on as relief was at hand. By September our troops had reclaimed Rovno, and peace negotiations had begun. I was demobbed with the rank of Colonel.

CHAPTER 9

RETURN TO ROVNO (1920)

As soon as I was able, I returned to the house in Rovno, still remarkably untouched by the battles fought in the streets of the town. I now had a chance to properly explore the house and found many personal items that had been left behind by the General and his family in their haste to leave. Unsure if they might return one day to reclaim any of these items, I decided to put them in the attic for safekeeping. There I found a treasure trove of relics from Imperial Russia: ancient weapons, including various guns, swords and sabres, military uniforms, old wire and horse-hair crinolines, laces, furs, and even a few old wooden toys. Only six years ago I had been part of that world, a world of high society balls and banquets, of elegant horse-drawn carriages, of palaces and royalty, of colour and grandeur. The contrast between my past and the present was all the more stark now that the dry summer months were over and the autumn rain had turned the unpaved streets into rivers of mud. The hunger and deprivation caused by six years of war were visible even to the most reluctant eye. The town was full of refugees from the east, some passing through, some hoping to settle here, their wagons loaded with belongings and family members. Barefooted children, carrying whatever bowls they could find, queued outside the soup kitchen.

Still reeling from the trauma of war, I found there were not many elementary schools open yet in the town, so it wasn't long before I located Sofia. I heard her before I saw her, in the distance walking behind me, her small-heeled shoes clicking on the cobble stones. When I glanced around to see who was walking behind me, I instinctively knew it was her even though she now wore her hair in the fashionable crimped bob. Amazingly, she instantly recognised me from our previous brief encounter, and her eyes lit up with undisguised pleasure. I took her hand to kiss in the old-fashioned way.

"So did these pianist hands become teacher's hands Sofia?" I asked.

"Yes. You remembered my name and came back as you promised," she almost whispered. "Now you must tell me your name and then we will be properly introduced."

My work entitled me to the use of a motor car so I invited her to go with me for a drive to the Horyn River where we might walk undisturbed. Snugly wrapped in a warm coat and with a shawl over her head, she gingerly climbed into the car, lightly resting her hand in mine, I can still recall the thrill of that moment. We drove as far as I dared on the muddy tracks and parked close to an orchard, already heavy with fruit. In a nearby meadow a group of children were hopping around a small bonfire that they had made.

"I expect they are roasting wild pears," said Sofia in her soft refined voice, "I do love wild pears myself," she added shyly. I told her that I wasn't sure that I knew the difference between wild pears and other kinds and discovered that she knew all about fruit of all kinds.

"Yes, I do know quite a lot about fruit, my father is quite an expert on the subject. He has travelled all over Europe, to France, Italy, and Holland, collecting unusual varieties of apples, pears and plums," she told me. "In fact," she added proudly, "He is such an expert on the propagation of fruit trees, and the introduction of different varieties into Poland, that he has written a book on the subject." She laughed then and apologised for boring on about fruit and said that I would have to hear it all over again when I met him for myself.

It wasn't long before I made the journey to Sofia's family estate. We had met up and gone for several long walks before this and it seemed to me that Sofia sensed that I did not wish to talk about the past. Instead, we talked about the future, the kind of future we hoped for our country and for ourselves.

Sofia's father was as I remembered him, a handsome man with a moustache and a small beard, and considerably older than his wife, Sofia's mother, to whom I was introduced along with her sister Hannah. He had been a Captain of Cavalry in the Austro-Hungarian Army at the time of the Austrian Emperor Franz Joseph and evidently ruled his household with strict military precision.

"Yes, well, don't dawdle," barked the Captain, "I have the bees to attend to."

"Bees?" I whispered questioningly in Sofia's ear.

"Yes, did I forget to mention it? Father keeps bees, he has about two hundred beehives," came the soft reply.

In the drawing room we drank tea together, Sofia's mother managing the samovar herself, and Sofia was commanded to play the piano. She played a few lyrical folksongs.

"Do you know any pieces by Chopin?" I had asked with a mix of hope and regret.

"Yes, I have studied a few pieces and perhaps one day I shall have the courage to play them for you, but not today," was the elusive reply for which I found myself surprisingly thankful. After drinking tea, we were marched outside where the Captain exhibited his orchard as if it were a military review. The trees had been planted in rows like soldiers on parade, and he clearly knew every single branch of every tree. The beehives were positioned in similar rows in the orchard. He escorted me to a large room that he had built for drying the fruit on a large scale and proudly demonstrated his particularly large variety of pears. I must have met with his approval as he not only gave me the grand tour of his estate but graciously granted me leave to court his daughter.

During one of my visits, Sofia told me more about her father, a man who I hoped to get to know well in the future.

"Father is from a family of engineers who built furnaces for iron and steel works, and one of their furnaces is used all over Europe. But he didn't want to go into the family business, and because his family lived in the Austrian partition of Poland, he joined the Austrian Army and was promoted to Captain. He retired when he was fifty-five. Mother was only sixteen when they married."

"Then how old is he now?" I asked interrupting. We worked out that he must already have been eighty-six!

"Anyway," continued Sofia, glancing up at me with twinkling eyes, "he got a job with his old commanding officer, a titled gentleman, with a large estate near Ostrog, which as you know is not far from here. In appreciation for his loyalty, my father was promised a large piece of land and forests. Unfortunately for father, the old officer went abroad and died while he was away but hadn't left a will, so father received nothing. But as you can see, he was able to buy himself this land and build a house, grow his fruit and care for his beloved bees," she finished with a happy lilt in her voice.

After the Treaty of Riga was signed the following March, we found ourselves living on the border with Soviet Ukraine. One day I brought Sofia to my house to have a look around, having persuaded Stanislaw's wife to accompany us and act as chaperone on the tour. There was a piano in the drawing room and Sofia almost ran up to it in excitement, only to be disappointed at how out-of-tune it had become.

"I shall make it my mission to get the piano tuned as soon as possible," I promised. "I will have to find somewhere to buy a violin," I added.

"Oh, can you play? Then we will be able to play duets — I always wished that Hannah had learned the violin instead of us both playing the piano," she said naively clapping her hands. We even explored up in the attic where Sofia pounced on the crinoline cages with great delight. She climbed into the wire cage and swung it from side to side like a little girl in her first party dress.

"These must have been so impractical to wear, but I'm sure they would have looked beautiful covered in taffeta or lace-covered silks," she said with a tone of regret, then climbing back out she began to rummage around amongst the old military relics. "What will you do with all these old weapons?" she asked, giving me a sideways glance, "they would be very dangerous for children…" I took the hint.

Sofia consented to marry me, I in my officer's uniform, she in white lace, long veil, and flowers. Sofia's father Joseph gave us his blessing before church in typical military fashion while her mother and sister wept. We were sprinkled with holy water, a candle was lit, and a crucifix kissed before processing to the church. After the ceremony, Sofia's mother presented us with the traditional large round loaf of bread decorated with salt, conjuring up so many memories - His Imperial Majesty the Tsar, Herbert Hoover, lost family, and friends - but here was a new beginning. Before long, on March 15th, 1923, a son was born to us, and then a daughter. I resumed architecture as a career, devoting my life to my family and to rebuilding Poland.

AUTHOR'S NOTES ON PART ONE, AND COPY OF TRANSCRIPTS (This is included for authenticity)

Viktor recounted his memoirs to his wife Mary in the year in which he was seventy which she typed up on an old mechanical typewriter. I was kindly given photocopies of the typed manuscript. I recorded two interviews with the couple in August 2019 and these two sources are the basis for this manuscript.

A copy of the first part of the typed manuscript is given below:

"My father, Jan, came from a wealthy family who owned a large estate near Kiev. The estate consisted of forests, rivers, lakes, and a vast amount of farmland. The estate was looked after by a huge staff and included a bakery, grain mill, sawmills, orchards and cultivated farmland.

My father was educated in St Petersburg as an architect.

When Tsarist Russia went to war with Austria and Prussia, his father was called up into the unit that guarded the Tsar and his family.

When Tsar Nicholas started to lose the war, he made the grave mistake of assuming personal command of the army. The Tsar had lost faith in his generals and tried to save the situation by assuming control himself. All his personal officers and guards (including my father) were sent to the front line, as the Tsar had more faith in them than in the officers already in position. Army discipline had started to crack up, as most of the officers were from wealthy families and had not received proper military training but had been promoted because of their wealth.

My father was sent to the front in command of a cavalry brigade responsible for the defence of bridges and other fortifications. During the fighting he was wounded in the head by a sword; the injury was serious, and he was sent back to the Lazaret Hospital in St Petersburg for treatment and convalescence. He stayed in hospital until the day the Tsar's army collapsed. As soon as he heard the news of the great defeat, he left hospital and decided to return to his father's home near Kiev. This was a very difficult journey as the Bolsheviks had already taken over, and anyone caught without papers was shot immediately – and especially members of the Tsar's defeated army. The revolution was in full swing and the whole country was in complete chaos. Father was arrested whilst trying to board a train. The revolutionaries always looked at a person's hands, and if they were clean and smooth, they instantly recognised the person as not being of working-class origins. Luckily for father, he was handed over to a Polish-speaking Commissar for interrogation. Father admitted his background and begged for help to return home.

The Commissar listened carefully and told father that he was in exactly the same position and was looking for a way to escape. He told him that, for the present time, he had survived by pretending to be 'from the people' and he eventually wanted to escape from the situation. He found father some civilian clothes and told him not to shave, and most importantly to keep his hands dirty and oily, and to wear coarse linen underwear. Most people were detected by their underwear and soft hands. He also found him a pair of very old shoes and a stick so that he could walk with a limp, and with all this help he disguised himself quite successfully.

On his journey home he was stopped by Bolsheviks on several occasions but managed to evade arrest. At that time, only one question was ever asked; if you did not answer that satisfactorily you were shot — you never had a second chance. Everyone was judged solely on his appearance and if you were dressed respectably and spoke with an educated accent, you automatically became an enemy of the people.

On nearing home, he heard that his father and mother had been murdered by the estate workers and the local rebels, as also had many other landowners in the area. The Kiev area of Russia was mostly inhabited by Polish landowners — the vast majority of whom were murdered by the revolutionaries and their lands confiscated by the government. When just outside his home, father was met by a loyal servant, who told him all that had happened to his parents. The servant secreted him into his home, where he was able to collect his father's hidden store of gold coins and make his escape into Poland. In those days Russia had only gold currency and as my grandfather never trusted banks, he kept his gold hidden in the cellars. There were always rumours that one day the government would replace gold currency with paper money and grandfather was very dubious of the honesty of the banks.

Father changed into his civilian clothes and carrying with him as much of the family gold as he could safely hide about his person, he walked through the forests into the eastern part of Poland, which was still occupied by Russian troops. At this time, General Pilsudski was organising an underground Polish army to fight the Russian Army of occupation, and my father *joined his brigade. Being an ex-officer from the Tsar's guard, he was immediately given a command and fought under General Pilsudski until the defeat of the Russian army in 1918. My father was then demobilised with the rank of Major, and following his earlier training as an architect, he was directed by the new Polish Government to take charge of building armament factories by the River Bug. Once again, Russia threatened Poland, and in 1922 father was recalled to the army, with the rank of Colonel, and after the successful battle against the Russian Marshall Budyonny, left the army, once again, and resumed his work as an architect, devoting his life to rebuilding Poland. About this time, he met and married a local teacher, Sophie, and they bought a large old house in Rovno and started a family, myself (Viktor) and my sister, Susannah.*

I only knew one grandfather – my mother's father – named Joseph. When I first remembered him, he was an extremely elderly man. He came from a well-known family of engineers who built furnaces for iron and steel works, and one of their furnaces was used all over Europe. Grandfather had not gone into the family business but had made the army his career. At that time, Poland was occupied by three countries, Austria, Prussia, and Russia, and as grandfather's family lived in the Austrian partition, he joined the Austrian army. He rose in the ranks and was a Captain in the Cavalry at the time of Emperor Franz Joseph's reign. He retired from the army at the age of fifty-five. His first job was with his old commanding officer, a titled man, with a large estate near Ostrog in eastern Poland. In appreciation of being a loyal worker, he had been promised a large piece of land and forests. Unfortunately for grandfather, his employer went abroad and whilst away from home he died. Not having made a will, grandfather received nothing for all his loyal service. When this happened, he bought himself a piece of land and decided to grow fruit as a hobby. He spent many months travelling all over Europe (including France, Italy, and Holland), collecting unusual varieties of apples, pears, and plums. He had a large house built amongst his orchards and soon married for the first time. He became such an expert on the propagation of fruit trees and the introduction of different varieties into the country, that he wrote a book on the subject.

The trees in the orchard were planted like rows of soldiers on parade, and he knew every single branch of every tree. In the orchards he kept about two hundred beehives, which produced honey for family use as well as for sale. As we lived quite close to him, we had unlimited supplies of honey and all varieties of fruit. In addition, he had built a room for drying fruit on a large scale, apples, pears, and plums. He grew the largest pears I have ever seen anywhere in Europe, with juice just like honey, but this particular variety would not keep, and they were subject to damage by wasps and bees because of their succulence,

Grandfather was a handsome man, with a moustache and small beard, and he married a very young lady of sixteen years of age. They had two daughters, one my mother and the other Aunt Hannah."

In interview, Viktor told me that his paternal grandparents, who lived in Zhuzolynka (phonetically presumed spelling) after the revolution, had been tortured and hung by the feet on a tree. He also told me that his father had bought the house in Rovno from a retired Russian General who emigrated to Paris, France, because of the Bolshevik threat. He said that his father had been able to pay cash and had bought the house "lock, stock and barrel."

Speaking about his maternal grandmother, Viktor told me: "*My grandma came from Russia. A long time ago, when the Russian territory was empty everywhere, they had a lot of land, and two million people were moved to Russia for the land. They settled down there. There were not enough people in Russia to build the country. They emigrated from Germany and the Czech Republic, maybe two hundred years ago. Russia and Germany were friends. Russia invited the people to help Russia; so, my grandmother was German.*" In the interview, Viktor told me that his maternal grandfather's family name was Martynovsky.

In Mary's typed account there are several historical inaccuracies regarding the post-revolution war period, that I have endeavoured to correct. To fill in the gaps, and to verify much of the detail, I have used a variety of sources, but mainly diaries that have thankfully been translated into English.

During the interviews, Mary showed me a photograph of the Tsar and Royal family with members of the Konvoy including General Grabbe. Viktor pointed to one of the Cossacks and told me that it was his father in the informal photograph taken by General Count Grabbe just before the official one that can be found in the book 'The Private World of the Last Tsar'. In a separate photograph of Herbert Hoover's visit to Warsaw in 1919, a Polish officer was pointed to and declared by Mary to be Viktor's father.

BRIEF BIOGRAPHIES OF NOTABLE PEOPLE:

Tsar Nicholas (II) Alexandrovich Romanov (1868-1918): Last Emperor of Russia, King of Congress Poland, and Grand Duke of Finland. He was executed by the Bolsheviks whilst in captivity in July 1918 along with his wife and all five children.

Dowager Empress Maria Feodorovna (1847- 1928) Mother of Tsar Nicholas II, wife of Alexander III of Russia and former Empress consort of Russia. She emigrated to Copenhagen and died in exile.

General Count Alexander Grabbe (1864-1947) In 1914 he was appointed commander of the Konvoy regiment — the Cossack unit that was the Tsar's elite guard. He served Nicholas II until his abdication on March 15, 1917. He emigrated to the United States and died in exile.

General Yuri Nikiforovich Danilov (1866-1937) General of Infantry in Imperial Russian Army; Quartermaster General; Chief of staff of the Northern Front; Commander of the 5th Army. After the October Revolution of 1917, he emigrated to Paris and died in exile.

General Lavr Georgiyevich Kornilov (1870-1918) Russian military intelligence officer and explorer. General in the Imperial Russian Army. He became commander of the anti-Bolshevik Russian volunteer army and was killed in action.

Marshal Jozef Klemens Pilsudski (1867-1935) Chief of State 1918-22; First Marshal of Poland from 1920. Minister of Military Affairs 1926-35. Born into a noble family in

Lithuania in the Russian Empire. He died of liver cancer whilst residing at the Belvedere Palace in Warsaw.

Ignacy Jan Paderewski (1860-1941 Internationally renowned Polish pianist and composer. Prime minister of Poland 1919 and Foreign Minister. Signatory of the Treaty of Versailles. Retired from politics in 1922. He emigrated to the United States and died in exile.

Jan Kowalewski Lt. Col. (1892-1965) Polish cryptologist and intelligence officer. Served in the Imperial Russian Army in the Polish 4th Rifle Division as chief of intelligence. He decrypted Soviet codes during the Polish-Soviet war – kept secret for over 70 years. Kowalewski's team were the first to crack the German Enigma cipher machine. He emigrated to the United Kingdom and died in exile.

Herbert Clark Hoover (1874-1964) 31st President of the United States. Head of the Commission for Relief in Belgium 1914. Head of US Food Administration 1917. Head of American Relief Administration 1918.

Lady Sybil Grey OBE (1882-1966) Second daughter to the 4th Earl Grey, philanthropist, and Voluntary Aid Detachment nurse. In 1915 she moved to Russia to establish the Anglo-Russian Hospital with Lady Muriel Paget.

ADDITIONAL HISTORICAL SOURCES:

The Private World of the Last Tsar. 1984. Edited by Paul and Beatrice Grabbe. Little, Brown & Co.

Thirteen years at the Russian court. 1921. Pierre Gilliard (1879-1962). Translated by F. Appleby Holt. George H Doran & Co.

Six Years at the Russian Court. 1906. M. Eagar. Charles L Bowman & Co.

The Diary of Nicholas II, 1917-18, An Annotated Translation. 1965. Kent D Price. University of Montana.

War and Revolution in Russia 1914-1917. 1919. General Basil Gourko. The Macmillan Company.

Nurse Writers of the Great War. 2016. Christine E Hallett. Nursing History and Humanities. Manchester University Press

Milton Keynes UK
Ingram Content Group UK Ltd.
UKHW040651220424
441549UK00004B/54